G GRAMMAR OALS

HANDBOOK FOR ENGLISH WRITING

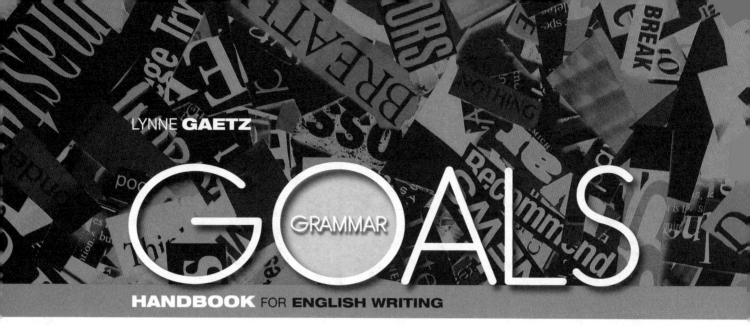

LYNNE **GAETZ**

G**OALS**
GRAMMAR

HANDBOOK FOR **ENGLISH WRITING**

PEARSON
Longman

1611 CRÉMAZIE BOULEVARD EAST, 10TH FLOOR, MONTRÉAL, QUÉBEC H2M 2P2
TELEPHONE: **1 800 263-3678**   FAX: **514 334-4720**
information@pearsonerpi.com   pearsonerpi.com

Managing Editor
Sharnee Chait

Editor
Lucie Turcotte

Copy Editor
Katya Epstein

Proofreader
Katie Shafley

Photo Research
Marie-Chantal Masson

Art Director
Hélène Cousineau

Graphic Design Coordinator
Karole Bourgon

Book and Cover Design / Layout
Valérie Deltour

Photo Credits

p. 2   © MikLav / shutterstock
p. 9   © robert cocquyt / iStockphoto
p. 13   © iStockphoto
p. 20   © BigStock
p. 25   © Tonylady / shutterstock
p. 30   © Megapress
p. 39   © Jeffrey Smith / iStockphoto
p. 47   © Bart van den Dikkenberg / iStockphoto
p. 57   © GetStock
p. 66   © BigStock
p. 74   © Tan Kian Khoon / shutterstock
p. 77   © Corbis
p. 86   © Dr. Heinz Linke / iStockphoto
p. 92   © Suzanne Tucker / shutterstock
p. 98   © Edward Hardam / iStockphoto
p. 107   © Corbis
p. 115   © Corbis

Registration of copyright: Bibliothèque et Archives nationales du Québec, 2010
Registration of copyright: Library and Archives Canada, 2010

Printed in Canada   4567890   HLN   16 15
ISBN 978-2-7613-3547-8   133547 ABCD   OF10

TABLE OF CONTENTS

UNIT 1

ACADEMIC AND BUSINESS LANGUAGE

 Standard English

Standard English is the common language generally used and expected in schools, businesses, and government institutions. It is grammatically correct and natural-sounding English. **Informal English** may be appropriate in a casual conversation, but it should not be used in academic or workplace communications.

■ Avoid Slang and Clichés

Slang is casual and even racy language that is used in informal situations. For instance, *dude* or *guy* are slang words for "man." **Clichés** are tired and overused expressions. For example, *He's hot under the collar* is a cliché meaning "He's angry." In the working world and in academic writing, use more formal language. Review the examples of informal and standard English.

Informal: The guy in the blue suit is my boss. He did some cool stuff at his previous company, but then the company went bust. He was totally bummed.

Standard: The man in the blue suit is my employer. He created some fascinating products at his previous company, but then the company went bankrupt. He was quite upset.

■ Use Standard Verb Forms

Review the list of informal and standard verb forms.

Informal	Standard
ain't	is/am/are not
gonna	going to
gotta	have to
have got to	have to
wanna	want to

TIP

Avoid Double Negatives

A double negative occurs when you combine a negative word such as *no* or *nothing* with a negative adverb such as *not*, *never*, *hardly*, or *seldom*. The result is a confusing sentence because the negative words cancel each other out.

To correct double negatives, remove one negative form or change *no* to *any*.

Double Negative	**Possible Corrections**
He doesn't have no money.	He has no money. He doesn't have any money.

EXERCISE 1

Edit the following paragraphs. Underline and replace informal language and non-standard verbs, and correct any double negatives. Make twenty corrections. (Note: each slang phrase counts as one error.)

EXAMPLE: The economy ~~gotta~~ *has to* improve.

1. Every year, many people wanna make money by investing in stocks. However, they got to be careful because buying stocks is similar to gambling. In September 2008, the United States government had to poke its nose in the affairs of Wall Street. Many investment funds tanked. Around the world, people freaked when they saw their stocks falling. Unfortunately, governments didn't do nothing until it was too late.

2. The collapse on Wall Street had a domino effect. Economies around the world suffered. Of course, a bunch of rich suits made fortunes by selling when the stock market was high and buying when the market was low. However, many average dudes lost their savings, and they wondered who was gonna take the blame. In fact, nobody did nothing heroic. The lack of accountability really bugged average citizens. Investment bank executives said it ain't their fault that the stock market fell. In the meantime, they didn't take no pay cuts even as their companies failed.

3. Over the course of the financial crisis, the American government contributed wads of dough to many large companies. The directors of the banks were super psyched when they heard that they would get financial help. However, regular taxpayers thought that the deal sucked big time.

4. The stock market collapse of 2008 taught investors an important lesson. If they are gonna invest in the stock market, they got to be careful about which investments they choose. These days, a lot of people have decided that they ain't going to invest in stocks no more.

Connotation versus Denotation

Words have literal meanings, but they also have emotional associations. A **denotation** is a word's direct meaning or dictionary definition. A **connotation** is a word's associated or secondary meaning. For example, *father* means "male parent." But the word *father* also has connotations. It may trigger feelings of security or resentment, depending on the person's experience with fathers. Additionally, some words have obvious positive or negative connotations. For example, *skinny* has a negative connotation and *slender* has a positive connotation.

EXERCISE 2

Decide if each word has a positive (+), negative (−), or neutral (0) connotation.

EXAMPLE: childish ⎯⎯ pure ⎯⎯ young ⎯⎯ innocent ⎯⎯ immature ⎯⎯

1. mutiny ____   riot ____   protest ____   disturbance ____
   revolution ____   rebellion ____

2. outgoing ____   social ____   talkative ____   friendly ____
   overbearing ____

3. sanctuary ____   home ____   shack ____   cottage ____
   slum ____   house ____

4. meticulous ____   perfectionist ____   anal ____   fussy ____
   thorough ____

5. terrorist ____   corporal ____   freedom fighter ____
   soldier ____   anarchist ____   hero ____

Underline the word in each pair that has a more positive connotation.

 EXAMPLE: demand   request

1. aggressive	assertive		**6.** snob	cultured
2. leader	boss		**7.** secretary	executive assistant
3. chef	cook		**8.** helper	mentor
4. shopper	customer		**9.** qualified	skilled
5. farmer	peasant		**10.** garbage collector	sanitation worker

Concise English

When writing in English, it is always better to be clear and **concise** (brief and to the point) rather than repetitive and wordy.

■ Avoid Wordiness

The main rule for most business and academic writing today is to get to the point. Avoid lengthy or repetitive phrases that can be more succinctly stated in a few words. If you are writing an academic paper, do not fill it with extra words simply to meet a length requirement. Not only do you risk boring your readers, but they may also miss your message. Review these examples of wordy expressions and substitutions.

Wordy or Outdated Expressions	Acceptable Substitutions
at this point in time	now, these days
due to the fact that	because
exceptions to the rule	exceptions
in order to	to
in this day and age	today, these days
in view of the fact that	because
it has come to my attention	I have learned
final outcome	outcome
for the duration of	for
for the reason that	because
permit me to say	(omit)
please be advised that	(omit)
small in size	small
the fact of the matter is	in fact (or omit it)
visible to the eye	visible
we wish to inform you	(omit)
will you be so kind as to	please
with the exception of	except

Also, avoid restating the obvious. For example, the next sentence is from an academic paper. Can you see the problem?

> In *The Handmaid's Tale*, Margaret Atwood investigates our human desire to create a utopia. In her novel, Atwood conveys the idea that the setting of the novel depicts a theocracy, which is a theocratic fascist state in which everyone must obey religious laws created by church leaders.

By deleting wordiness and by removing information that is already implied, the excerpt becomes clearer.

> In *The Handmaid's Tale*, Margaret Atwood investigates people's desire to create a utopia. The novel is set in a fascist state controlled by religious leaders.

EXERCISE 4

Correct the following sentences by removing or modifying words.

> **EXAMPLE:** At that ~~point in~~ time, the economy was experiencing a downturn.

1. Due to the fact that the brokers were dishonest, many investors lost money.

2. The fact of the matter is that there were not enough regulations to govern the American financial industry.

3. For several years, money lenders encouraged unemployed or low-income families to take out loans that were large in size.

4. It has come to my attention that the problems in the mortgage market were not visible to the eye.

5. For the purpose of solving the crisis, the US government bailed out Wall Street investment banks.

6. In the final analysis, there were many precautions the government should have taken.

7. Walter Simpson, an essayist, wrote an essay about the financial crisis.

8. In his essay, Simpson blamed the government. He criticized some governments around the world for removing regulations on the financial industry.

■ Avoid Repetition

To make your writing more vivid and interesting, avoid repeating the same terms over and over. For example, it is unnecessary to repeat the word *city* several times in a paragraph, when terms such as *municipality* and *urban centre* would convey the same meaning. Review the following two examples of the same paragraph. Notice that **synonyms** (words that mean the same thing) help improve the second paragraph.

> Dull, repetitive: In 2008, **stock** prices around the world **fell**. The **falling** of some US banks initiated the **fall** of the **stock** markets. People panicked as they saw their **stocks fall**. Many sold their **stocks**, causing the **stocks** to **fall** further.

Detailed, uses synonyms: In 2008, **stock** prices around the world **fell**. The **collapse** of some US banks initiated the **descent** of the **financial markets**. People panicked as they saw their **investments plummet**. Many sold their **portfolios**, causing the **value of shares** to **fall** further.

■ Avoid Vague Words

When you proofread your work, revise words that are too vague. **Vague words** lack precision and detail. Instead, use more vivid and specific vocabulary. To create vivid language, you can do the following:

• Modify your nouns. If your noun is vague, make it more specific by adding one or more adjectives. You could also replace the noun with a more specific term.

    Vague: the man
    Vivid: the stock broker   the confident lawyer

• Modify your verbs. Use more vivid, precise verbs. You could also use adverbs.

    Vague: talk
    Vivid: whisper   shout incoherently

• Include more details. Add more information to make the sentence more complete. (Avoid wordiness. Your goal is to make your writing more precise but not repetitive.)

    Vague: Mr. Roy was a bad man.
    Precise: Mr. Roy was a corrupt and greedy bank chairman.

    Vague: The advertisement is good.
    Precise: The magazine advertisement, with its colourful graphics and bold font, has a simple but funny message.

TIP

Synonyms

When you type in Word, remember that you can right-click on a term to find a synonym menu. Also, to view an online dictionary and thesaurus, visit a site such as ldoceonline.com or dictionaryreference.com.

EXERCISE 5

Replace each word with at least three synonyms. Use a dictionary or thesaurus, if necessary.

    EXAMPLE: to think   *imagine, believe, consider, reflect, ponder*

            employee   *worker, staff member, labourer, assistant*

1. to change   _____

2. to remove   _____

3. to complain   _____

4. boss   _____

5. factory   _____

6. store   _____

EXERCISE 6

Replace five of the underlined words with synonyms to make the paragraph more varied and interesting.

Yesterday, I talked with my financial advisor. We talked about my investment portfolio.

Then we talked about the best strategy to follow. In another room, we heard

Mrs. Beacon talking loudly. She was very angry and we could hear her talking.

We decided to postpone our meeting and talk another time.

EXERCISE 7

Replace the familiar words in the parentheses and add more specific details. You can use your dictionary or thesaurus if you need help.

EXAMPLE: The weather was (bad) _____cool and overcast_____.

1. On a (nice day) _____, the

   politician entered the courtroom.

2. The politician is (very bad) _____.

3. During his years in office, the politician accepted (things) _____

   _____ from city contractors.

4. The judge was (nice) _____.

5. During the questioning by the prosecutor, the politician (was nervous) _____

   _____.

6. The lawyer had (a lot of stuff) _____

   on his desk.

Considering Your Audience and Purpose

The English language is not static; it evolves. New vocabulary is introduced, other words fall out of favour, and sometimes grammatical notions change. When you use English in academic, professional, and business environments, be aware of current language trends. Ensure that your language fits your audience and purpose for writing. If you use inappropriate language, you can undermine your credibility.

For example, in the past, overly formal and flowery language was the norm in both business and personal writing. Read this example from a letter sent in 1824.

> I expect that this correspondence shall find you in most excellent health. I shall now bid farewell and desire you to remember my best respects to all my enquiring friends.
> I remain with high respect
> Your most particular friend,
> Daniel T. Potts

Some languages use such flowery language, but it is not appropriate in English. English—especially business English—is direct and concise. Review how the antiquated letter, printed above, appears in current standard English.

> I hope you're well. Please send my regards to our mutual friends.
> All the best,
> Daniel T. Potts

Today, with instant messaging and emails, language may be overly informal. In the following text message, the abbreviations, misspellings, and lack of capitalization would not be appropriate in an academic or workplace setting.

> hey :)
> how ru? i'm in ur class. can u help with my essay? b4 i rite, what is # words? dunno if im on the rite track :/
> gtg mark
> btw will cu in class

TIP

Jargon

Certain professions have particular language styles and vocabulary. **Jargon**—language used in a specific profession and not easily understood by others—is fine when writing documents for your field of study. However, when writing for a larger audience, use layman's terms—or ordinary, everyday language.

> Jargon: The man suffered from a **periorbital hematoma**.
> Everyday English: The man suffered from a **black eye**.

EXERCISE 8

Edit the following selections. Make them into concise English.

1. The following excerpt is from a letter written in 1854. Rewrite the sentences to make them contemporary. You can shorten and simplify them.

> I beg to say that I am well acquainted with bookkeeping business and have sufficient knowledge of French to conduct correspondence in that language with ease. Trusting I may hear from you, and thanking you in advance for any information you may afford me regarding the above, I am, with the greatest respect, very sincerely yours.

_____

_____

_____

_____

2. The following selection is from a text message. Rewrite the sentences in direct and standard English.

> crazy busy at work think I took on 2 much stuff gotta go. cu 2nite

_____

_____

3. Rewrite the following sentence to remove the jargon. You can shorten and simplify the sentence.

> When hot transmission fluid builds up in the motor vehicle's radiator core, the pressure valve in the cap may open and allow coolant to overflow.

_____

_____

_____

_____

UNIT Review

Answer the following questions. If necessary, go back and review the appropriate section.

1. What is wordiness? _____

2. Provide examples of slang. _____

3. Correct the errors in the following sentences.

a) Jason Smith doesn't know nothing about selling.

b) Unfortunately, Smith got a lot of debts.

c) Every week, he sells stuff on eBay.

d) For the purpose of reducing his debts, he has sold a lot of his clothing.

e) To sell his sofa, he used a photo that really bites.

f) Honestly, nobody is gonna buy his sofa.

FINAL REVIEW

PART A

Underline and correct errors in grammar and remove examples of slang or wordiness. Make ten corrections.

EXAMPLE: The clients thought that the site was way cool.
fascinating

1. Back in 1995, Pierre Omidyar was a software developer. He wrote the code for AuctionWeb, which would evolve into eBay. For the purpose of testing his site, Omidyar advertised a broken laser pointer. He didn't think nobody would wanna buy it. Imagine his surprise when someone offered $14.83 for the item. Omidyar wasn't gonna accept the bid, and he reminded the buyer that the laser pointer was broken. The buyer said that he gotta collection of broken laser pointers! At that moment, Omidyar was all fired up because he knew that his idea would be successful. Since then, he has repeatedly seen that people will buy stuff online.

2. At that point in time, Omidyar had a web domain called Echo Bay. He shortened the name to eBay. Due to the fact that he hired competent people to help him, the website grew like crazy. Three years later, Omidyar was a billionaire.

PART B

Replace five of the underlined words with synonyms to make the paragraph more varied and interesting.

3. Eric needs to <u>change</u> his attitude. When he answers the phone, he should <u>change</u> his tone of voice. He always sounds annoyed. Maybe he can <u>change</u> the way that he deals with stress. Right now, he gets angry too easily. Perhaps if he <u>changes</u> the way that he looks at problems, he can find constructive ways to deal with them. Also, Eric should stop <u>complaining about</u> his job. He <u>complains about</u> the hours. He even <u>complains about</u> the uniform.

UNIT 2

PRONOUNS, PLURALS, AND COMPARISONS

 Problems with Pronouns

Over the years, you have undoubtedly learned a lot about pronouns. Perhaps there are still some errors that you make. Review the following points.

■ Pronoun-Antecedent Agreement

Pronouns can replace the subject or object in a sentence. A pronoun must agree with its **antecedent**, which is the word that the pronoun refers to. In the example, *the lawyers* is the antecedent for *them*.

> subject   object
> Rob and **I** spoke to <u>the lawyers</u>. Rob asked **them** many questions.

Be careful when a pronoun is paired with another noun. A simple way to determine the correct pronoun is to say the sentence with just one pronoun.

> The lawyers asked Rob and (I or me) to make another appointment.
>
> Possible choices: The lawyers asked **I** … / The lawyers asked **me** …
> Correct answer: The lawyers asked Rob and **me** to make another appointment.

■ Pronouns in Comparisons

When a pronoun follows a comparison that uses *than* or *as*, ensure that you use the correct subject or object pronoun. To verify that your pronoun is correct, complete the thought.

> I enjoy medical shows more than (**he** or **him**).
>
> Complete the thought: I enjoy medical shows more than **he** (enjoys medical shows).

■ Pronouns in Prepositional Phrases

In a prepositional phrase, the words following the preposition are always objects, so use the object pronoun form.

> **Between you** and **me**, the hospital waiting room is too crowded.
> The doctor will discuss the diagnosis **with us**.

■ Indefinite Pronouns

Indefinite pronouns such as *someone, nothing, anything, everybody, neither,* and *either* are singular. Use a singular pronoun when referring to them. (A complete list of singular indefinite pronouns appears on page 91 in Unit 10.

> In the women's ward, **nobody** could have **her** own room.
> **Neither** of us has **his** own car.

Note: If the gender of the subject is unknown, or if the subject is both genders, use the male and female pronoun. If the sentence appears awkward, simply change the subject to the plural form.

> Incorrect: **Everybody** must ask **their** visitors to leave.
> Solution: **Everybody** must ask **his or her** visitors to leave.
> Better solution: **The patients** must ask **their** visitors to leave.

In sentences containing the expressions *one of the* or *each of the,* the subject is the indefinite pronoun *one* or *each.* You must use a singular pronoun to refer to the subject.

> **One** of the accountants embezzled money from **her** client.

■ Reflexive Pronouns

When using reflexive pronouns (those ending in *-self* or *-selves*), ensure that the pronoun reflects back on the antecedent or person doing the action.

> Error: Today **I** interviewed David Foster to learn a little bit more about **himself**.
> (David is not doing the action, I am.)
> Correction: Today I interviewed David Foster to learn a little bit more about **him**.
> **I** conducted the interview by **myself**.

EXERCISE 1

Underline the correct pronoun in parentheses.

> **EXAMPLE:** My brother and (me / I) are in the same program.

1. My brother and (I / me) are studying to become nurses and are in the final year of (our / ours) program. This year, (he / him) and (I / me) are receiving practical experience in a hospital. Everybody in my nursing program has to pay for (our / their / his or her) own uniform and supplies. For example, the new stethoscopes in that box are for my classmates and (me / I / myself).

2. My brother Daniel is a good student. Sometimes the professor asks (he / him) and (I / me) to stay late. For example, today we will work an extra shift at the hospital. I am not sure if we should prepare the new patients by (myself / ourself / ourselves). Also my brother and (I / me) work on weekends. The supervisor usually asks (we / us / ourselves) to work on the children's ward. The children like my brother better than (I / me) because he is like a clown. Our friends Antonio and Mark occasionally work with us. Neither of (they / them) has (his / their) nursing degree.

3. My best friend, Carolina, is a better nursing student than (me / I). Between you and (I / me), I sometimes feel uncomfortable around sick people. My parents recently asked my brother and (I / me) if we were sure about our career choices. However, I tell (me / myself) that I will get used to this field. I will be proud of (me / myself) when I finish this program.

■ Pronoun Shift

When writing, ensure that your pronouns are consistent. For instance, if you refer to people in general, do not suddenly shift to *you* or *we*.

his or her

Everyone should finish ~~their~~ work.

Pronoun shifts can also occur within a paragraph.

their

People often eat too much sugar. Sugar is not good for ~~your~~ health.

2

EXERCISE 2

Underline and correct six pronoun shifts in the paragraph.

their

EXAMPLE: People should not use cellphones because radiation can enter your brain.

Cellphones are bad for people. Consumers must be careful because the more you use a phone, the greater your risks are. When someone talks on a phone, microwaves can penetrate our skull. Also, Dr. Kjell Mild believes that there is a link between cancer and cellphone radiation. Some studies show that patients have developed brain tumours after long-term cellphone exposure, so we should be careful. When someone talks on a cellphone, they should speak quickly and then hang up. Also, citizens should not buy cellphones for children, especially when you know the dangers.

■ Avoiding *I* and *You*

In some essays, the pronouns *I* and *you* are unavoidable. For instance, if you are narrating a story about a personal experience, you would use *I*, and if you are telling the reader the steps to take to complete a process, it makes sense to use *you*. However, in most academic writing, such pronouns should be avoided. In the first example, the underlined words should be removed or modified. The second example shows academic writing.

Not academic: <u>I believe that</u> energy drinks are bad for <u>your</u> health. Such drinks have extremely high levels of caffeine and can raise <u>your</u> blood pressure and dehydrate <u>your</u> body. <u>In my opinion</u>, <u>you</u> should avoid using them as a way to stay alert.

Academic: Energy drinks are bad for people's health. Such drinks have extremely high levels of caffeine and can raise blood pressure and cause dehydration. Consumers should avoid using the drinks as a way to stay alert.

Edit the following student paragraph by removing or modifying any forms of the pronouns *I* and *you*. Use a variety of replacement words.

There is
EXAMPLE: ~~I will talk about~~ a serious problem in our society.

I am very worried about tasers. Taser International claims that the weapons are not

harmful when used properly, but facts show otherwise. If you are hit with a taser,

you can be injured or even killed. A single jolt can disrupt your muscle control and

overstimulate your sensory system. In my opinion, police officers underestimate the

dangerous effects of the stun guns. I think that the death of a Polish immigrant in

Vancouver by taser could have been avoided. The weapons can kill you, and so

I truly believe that their use should be restricted.

Plurals

Plural forms can be complex. Review the following points.

- Use a singular noun after *each* and *every*. Use a plural noun after *one of*.
  <u>Every</u> **person** in the company is important.
  <u>One of</u> our biggest **problems** is employee absenteeism.

- Do not use *this* or *that* to refer to a plural item. Use *these* or *those* instead. (*That* and *those* refer to items or events that are distant or are in the past.)

Singular	**Plural**
this study	**these** studies
that problem	**those** problems

  When the Berlin Wall fell, **those** were very exciting days.

- Some nouns appear only in plural form. The object or idea being described might have two or more parts but is considered a singular entity. Use a plural verb to refer to these nouns.

binoculars	congratulations	glasses	proceeds	scissors
clothes	credentials	goods	savings	shorts

  My <u>clothes</u> **are** dirty. His <u>glasses</u> **are** in his pocket.

- Some nouns have a plural form but a singular meaning. Use the singular form of the verb with these nouns.

economics	mathematics	news	physics	politics

  <u>Physics</u> **is** complicated. The <u>news</u> **is** full of stories about the crisis.

- Some nouns are borrowed from foreign languages and keep the plural form of the original language.

Singular	**Plural**
cris**is**	cris**es**
criteri**on**	criteri**a**
graffit**o**	graffit**i**

  The **criteria** changed after we did some **analyses**.

© PEARSON LONGMAN • REPRODUCTION PROHIBITED

TIP

Adjectives are never plural.

Adjectives modify or provide information about nouns. Sometimes nouns act like adjectives. Always use the singular form of adjectives.

dollar
Mr. Kim created a million-<s>dollars</s> business.

2

EXERCISE 4

Underline and correct fifteen plural errors.

countries

EXAMPLE: Many <u>country</u> require visas.

1. Chantal wants to travel to others countries to learn new languages. One of the main reason she wants to study languages is that she hopes to become a translator. She will not visit countries that have political crisis because she is not interested in politic.

2. Chantal wants to learn Spanish and Italian because she thinks this languages will be easy to learn. First, Chantal wants to study Italian, so she will go to Italy and take course, and she will also practise speaking in publics places. She loves meeting her Italian friends in cafés, museum, and park, and she knows that this type of meetings are useful.

3. She will withdraw her saving from the bank, and then she will buy a six-hundred-dollars plane ticket to Rome. Every Italians that she meets will help her learn practicals language skills.

■ Non-Count Nouns

Many nouns in English have no plural form and cannot be counted. For instance, you cannot say *I need two informations*. Instead, you would have to say *I need some information* or *I need two pieces of information*. Review some common non-count nouns.

advice	equipment	knowledge	research
change (money)	evidence	luck	snow
clothing	hair	luggage	software
education	health	machinery	steam
effort	help	music	traffic
electricity	homework	proof	violence
energy	information	radiation	work

To refer to more than one item, put *pieces of* or *types of* before the noun. The non-count noun remains singular.

> I need three **pieces of** <u>information</u> from you.
> I listen to several **types of** <u>music</u>.

Underline and correct the plural error in each sentence. If the sentence is correct, write "C" in the space provided.

> **EXAMPLE:** He put a lot of <u>efforts</u> into his work. _____*effort*_____

1. The doctor didn't give me much advices after he wrote the prescription. _____

2. The factory has several sophisticated types of equipments. _____

3. We completed the survey questions, and we developed several hypothesis regarding the results. _____

4. Although there is no cure for cancer, scientists have done a lot of researches. _____

5. Mr. Blair requires some additional information about the project, and then he might provide some funding. _____

6. Scientists have contributed to human knowledges about many diseases, and ailments such as smallpox have been eradicated. _____

Adjectives and Adverbs

An adjective modifies a noun, and an adverb modifies a verb.

>   adjective noun
> Adjective: She is a very **quiet** <u>person</u>.
>
>   verb   adverb
> Adverb: She <u>works</u> **quietly**.

Review the following rules about adjective and adverb forms.

- **Adjective form:** Remember that nouns can function like adjectives when placed before other nouns.

  >   **year-old**
  > The twenty-~~years-old~~ man was hired.

- **Adjective order:** Adjectives appear before the noun they are modifying (*the innocent man*), or after the verb *be* (*he is innocent*).

  >   **two and a half** <u>years</u>
  > I've been in my program for ~~two years and a half~~.

- **Adverb form:** Always modify verbs with an adverb. Many adverbs end in *-ly*. Also, use *really* (instead of *real*) to modify another adverb.

  >   **really quietly**
  > Jessica spoke ~~real quiet~~ during her presentation.

T I P

Good and *Well*

Use *good* to modify a noun and *well* to modify a verb.

> The doctor has a **good** reputation because she treats her patients very **well**.

Exception: Use *well* to describe a person's health.

> The five-year-old boy does not feel **well**.

EXERCISE **6**

Underline and correct ten errors with adjectives or adverbs.

EXAMPLE: That nurse walks very <u>quick</u>. *(quickly)*

Accountants are very practicals people. Evan wants to be an accountant really bad.

He loves working with numbers and he thinks that accounting can be a rewarding

career. He would make a candidate superb. First, he learns things quick. Also, he has

worked as a junior tax accountant for one year and a half. He did his job quite good,

and his employers were pleased with him. Therefore, he is extreme comfortable in

a business environment. Finally, he is very sociable and communicates easy with

others people. He is very friendly, speaks good, and has a good sense of humour.

■ Comparative Forms

Be careful when comparing items with adjectives and adverbs. Review the following
points.

- **Comparatives:** Use *than* after a comparison. Add *–er* to the ends of one-syllable
  adjectives and adverbs or to the ends of two-syllable words ending in *–y* (*easier than*).
  Place *more* before other adjectives and adverbs of two or more syllables.

  > Skydiving is **riskier than** cycling. Adam is **more prepared than** Erica.

- **Superlatives:** Use *the* and add *-st* to the ends of short adjectives and adverbs and
  to two-syllable words ending in *–y*. Place *most* before adjectives and adverbs of two
  or more syllables.

  > Children are the **most active**, and adolescent females are **the laziest**, according
  > to our survey.

Exception: While *the* is normally used in superlative rather than comparative forms,
the following type of two-part expression uses *the* with the comparative form.
The second part is the result of the first part.

> **The more** you exercise, **the better** you will feel.

- **Expressing equality:** Use *as … as* or *the same as* when two items are equal.

  > Men view art **as** often **as** women. They have **the same** habits **as** women.

Comparisons with Adverbs

When comparing two actions, ensure that you use adverbs and not adjectives.

more nicely

Ellen writes <u>nicer</u> than Simon.

EXERCISE **7**

Underline and correct ten errors with adjective and adverb forms.

as

EXAMPLE: The United States has the same literacy rate <u>than</u> Canada.

1. Some bone diseases are worst then others. Osteoporosis is one of the worse bone diseases. By about age thirty-five, all adults lose some bone mass, and as people age, bone deteriorates rapidly. With osteoporosis, bones break easier than previously.

2. Women lose bone mass quicker after menopause then before. Some people become more shorter than they were in their youth because bone disease can cause the vertebrae in the back to collapse. For example, Marilyn Simpco is two inches and a half shorter than she was before.

3. Definitely, the more bone loss a person has, the most pain he or she will feel. Getting adequate exercise and calcium are the most effective ways to maintain bone density. Taking calcium pills is as effective than drinking milk. Both are wise choices.

■ Special Forms

Many, Few, Fewer, and Fewest

With count nouns, use *many, a few, very few, fewer*, and *fewest*. (Remember that you can place a number before count nouns: *twenty employees*.)

My friend has **many debts**. The bank laid off a **few employees**, although it laid off **fewer employees** than some other institutions. It had the **fewest layoffs** in the industry.

Much, Little, Less, and Least

With non-count nouns, use *much, a little, very little, less*, and *least*. (You cannot put a number directly before a non-count noun.)

David needs a **little advice**. He doesn't have **much information** about bankruptcy laws. He has **less knowledge** about bankruptcy laws than I do. In fact, he is the **least informed** person that I know.

Complete the sentences comparing and contrasting Canada and the United States. Choose words from the lists below. Some words can be used more than once.

few	fewer	fewest	little	less	least

1. The United States has _____ land than Canada does. However, Canada

   has _____ people than the United States does. If you add England to the

   list, Canada has the _____ people of all three nations, and England has

   the _____ amount of land of the three places.

2. The United States has _____ senators than Canada does. Canada has

   _____ members of the House than the United States does.

3. I need a _____ more information about Canada and the United States.

   I have a _____ friends who live in New York.

many	much	more	most

4. Canada has too _____ politicians. When you consider the difference

   in population, Canada has _____ politicians per one thousand people

   than the United States has. I believe that too _____ money is paid

   to government leaders.

UNIT Review

Answer the following questions. If necessary, go back and review the appropriate section.

1. Underline and correct five errors in pronoun forms.

   EXAMPLE: My brother and me love science.

   Our family dentist always treated my sister and I very well. My sister would get

   more scared than me. The dentist was very gentle with her. After each visit, he

   asked ourselves if we would like to have a toothbrush. With ours, he was always

   very kind. In our family, everybody has their own colour of toothbrush.

2. Underline and correct the error in each sentence. Then write which grammatical rule was being broken.

a) The twenty-years-old students were invited to the seminar.

Rule: _____

b) We conducted some researches about drinking and driving.

Rule: _____

c) Few things are as frightening than an appointment with a dentist.

Rule: _____

d) I learn languages easier than my sister does.

Rule: _____

FINAL REVIEW

PART A

Underline the appropriate word in parentheses.

1. Everyone must choose a job that (they / he or she) can feel passionate about. Some believe that police work is more dangerous (then / than) other occupations. However, being an electrician is as dangerous (than / as) being a police officer.

2. Electricians risk their lives when working on high-power wires. For instance, my cousin Gary is an electrician. In the summer of 2009, (he / him) and his colleague were working on a project. Gary fell from an electrical pole, and he hurt (hisself / himself / him). Every (times / time) he stands, he feels pain. Gary often asks my sister and (I / me) to visit him. My sister goes to see him more often than (I / me) because she lives near him.

3. Police officers have (less / fewer) fatalities than many other workers. On a list of the fifteen most dangerous jobs, police work is only number 11. One of the most dangerous (job / jobs) is fishing. It has the (higher / most high / highest) rating and is considered dangerous because there is a risk of drowning. Loggers have the second (more / most) dangerous job. The main reason is the risk of being hit by a falling object.

4. Each year, (fewer / less) people become loggers than before because of paper recycling. (Less / Fewer) paper is created from trees, and more paper is made of recycled material. Every (person / people) should recycle paper.

PART B

Underline and correct ten errors in plural, adjective, or adverb forms.

EXAMPLE: I have as many courses *than* my brother. as

5. The less dangerous job in the world is librarian. However, librarians do not have an easy job. In fact, they work real hard.

6. For instance, Elena is the head librarian at our local library, and she does her job good. She gives me a lot of advices. Whenever I need some informations for an assignment, she helps me.

7. The penalty for having a library debt is quite severe. Unfortunately, I lost a book and had to pay for it. It was the worse book I had ever read, yet it was a 95-dollars book! After that experience, I borrowed less books from the library.

8. Elena speaks quicker than her colleagues, but Elena is really the most friendliest person in the library. She is one of the nicest people I have ever met.

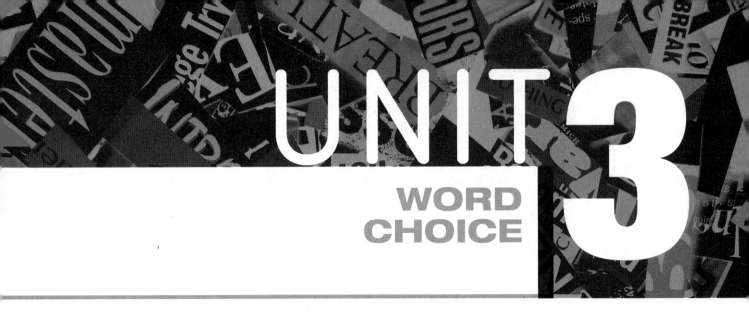

UNIT 3

WORD CHOICE

 Commonly Confused Words

Carefully review the following list of words that are often confused.

Term	Meaning	Example
accept	to receive or to admit	I **accept** responsibility for the loss.
except	excluding or other than	Everyone **except** my father is pleased.
advice	suggestion (noun)	I should have listened to my parents' **advice**.
advise	to suggest (verb)	My parents always **advise** me to stay in school.
affect	to influence (verb)	The long cold winter **affects** my mood.
effect	the result of something (noun)	The overcast weather has a bad **effect** on me.
aloud	spoken audibly	Please read the story **aloud** so the others can hear you.
allowed	permitted	We are not **allowed** to enter the defence building.
conscience	a personal sense of right or wrong	The thief had no **conscience**.
conscious	to be aware or to be awake	He is **conscious** that he broke the law. Luckily, his victim was still **conscious** after the attack.
council	assembly of leaders	We took our complaint to the city **council**.
counsel	advice; to advise; legal advisor	The accountant **counselled** me to reduce my spending. I will heed his **counsel**.
personal	private	The thief has some **personal** problems.
personnel	employees or staff	The department will hire new **personnel**.
principal	most important; school director	The **principal** reason I left is because of the salary.
principle	rule; standard	Matt has strong **principles** and would never cheat.
sale	a reduced price	There will be a **sale** tomorrow.
sell	to receive money in exchange for something	I plan to **sell** my car.
succeed	to do well in an endeavour (verb)	I hope to **succeed** in college.
success	achievement (noun)	I plan to have a lot of **success** in my field.

Term	Meaning	Example
though	although; even though	**Though** I tried hard, I failed.
thorough	complete; executed with accuracy	The doctor did a very **thorough** analysis of my condition.
through	in one side and out the other; finished	Go **through** the tunnel to get to the office. I am **through** for the day.
throughout	during the whole period; everywhere in a place	We worked on the project **throughout** the night. We searched for our notes **throughout** the house.
weather	atmospheric conditions	The **weather** is cloudy and cold today.
whether	introduces a clause; if	I'm not sure **whether** I should become an artist or a writer.
which	introduces a clause with additional information; question word	We are not sure **which** exit to take. **Which** one would you recommend?
witch	person with magical powers	In Salem, a young woman was accused of being a **witch**.

EXERCISE **1**

Fill in the blanks with words from the lists.

through	thorough	though	throughout

1. My best friend, Samuel, went _____ the same program as I did. Simon received very good grades in his courses even _____ he never worked very hard. I always suspected that he was lazy, but he apparently does very _____ research. In fact, _____ his university years, he was always an A student.

succeed	success

2. Samuel has recently found a job as a medical researcher, and I hope he has great _____. Honestly, I would also like to _____ in my career. However, I also hope that I am a _____ in my private life. To me, _____ is about more than just money. I want to _____ as a husband and father.

advise	advice	accept	except

3. Victoria needs some career _____. Her friends often _____ her to become a violinist. However, in her family, nobody _____ her mother thinks that it is a good idea. Victoria hopes that a music school will _____ her application.

| whether | weather | affect | effect |

4. Victoria is not sure _____ or not it is wise to hope for a musical career. She does not practise very often, and she wonders if her laziness will _____ her progress. Some people believe that nothing will _____ a truly talented person. However, most experts believe that a lot of practice has a very positive _____ on one's performance.

EXERCISE 2

Underline the appropriate word in parentheses.

1. Many houses are for (sell / sale) in our city. Cristina and Andrea (sell / sale) real estate. They are not (aloud / allowed) to charge more than a 7 percent commission. Today, they want to (sell / sale) a house in the suburbs. The potential buyer, Mr. Lee, is whispering to his wife. He is not speaking (aloud / allowed) because he doesn't want the agents to hear him.

2. I work in human resources and I hire (personal / personnel) for some city departments. Recently, I spoke with an administrator on the city (counsel / council) about the zoning problem. Mrs. Fleury is a (personal / personnel) friend of mine. My children used to babysit her children, so sometimes I (counsel / council) her about parenting issues.

Prepositions

Prepositions cannot easily be translated, and there are no sweeping rules that cover all prepositions. Listed below are some tricky prepositions that students often misuse.

Since **or** *For*

Use *since* when you are referring to a specific past time.

> I haven't heard from my brother **since** <u>last Friday</u>.
> We haven't played hockey **since** <u>we were children</u>.

Use *for* when you are referring to a quantity of time (a number of hours, days, weeks, months, and so on).

> We have been in this house **for** <u>twelve years</u>.
> I've been waiting for you **for** <u>a long time</u>!

To

Use *to* after verbs that suggest movement.

> We <u>went</u> **to** Morocco. Then we <u>drove</u> **to** the hotel.

© PEARSON LONGMAN • REPRODUCTION PROHIBITED

24 GRAMMAR GOALS

■ Prepositional Expressions

Many nouns, verbs, and adverbs are usually followed by certain prepositions. Memorize the following prepositional expressions.

afraid of	capable of	participate in	scared of
angry at/with	depend on	pay for *	search for
apologize for/to	different from	prepare for *	similar to
ask for *	familiar with	proud of	sorry for
aware of	interest in *	rely on	specialize in
believe in *	look at	responsible for	sure about/of

*These verbs can also be followed directly by a name or pronoun, but the meaning changes. For instance, *ask him* does not mean the same thing as *ask for him*.

Toni was **responsible for** the accident.
They **depend on** science to answer difficult questions.

EXERCISE 3

Underline the correct word in parentheses.

EXAMPLE: I will participate (on / <u>in</u>) a conference next month.

1. I am not really scared (of / at) success, but sometimes I depend (of / on) others to support me. For example, at my part-time job, I am responsible (of / for) several new employees, but I really rely (in / on / at) my colleague, Jane, to help me. In the past, I have sometimes been rude to Jane, but I have apologized (of / for / to) my bad behaviour.

2. I have a twin, but I am not similar (at /of / to) him. I am more introverted, and he is more outgoing. In fact, I am very different (to / from / of) him. He is not sure (about / to / on) his future plans, but I have very clear career goals. I want to be an environmental biologist. I really believe (of / in / on) global warming, and I want to do my part to help.

3. Next year, I will go (to / at / nothing) Concordia University and I will specialize (in / on) biology. I will also write a letter to the dean proving that I am capable (of / for) doing hard work. I am very interested (of / on / in) that field.

■ Phrasal Verbs

Sometimes a verb can be followed by various prepositions, and each combination has a specific meaning. Such verb-preposition combinations are called phrasal verbs. There are over a thousand phrasal verbs. Review some of the most common ones.

Phrasal Verb	Meaning	Phrasal Verb	Meaning
act up	behave improperly	give away	give something for free
back up	make copies (computer term)	give up	surrender; to stop a habit
break down	stop working; collapse	hand in	submit work
break in	use force to enter a locked place	hang out with	spend time with
break up	end a relationship	hang up	end a phone conversation
brush up (on)	review	lay off	dismiss an employee because there isn't enough work
call back	return a phone call	look after	take care of
call off	cancel	look for	search for
check in	register at a hotel	look into	investigate
check out	register out of a hotel; investigate	look up	find information in a book or computer
cut back (on)	reduce the use of something	put away	return to its proper place
drop by	visit without an appointment	put off	postpone
drop off	stop to give something to someone	put on	place on the body (put on shoes, etc.)
drop out (of)	quit school	take after	resemble
fill in/out	complete a form	take back	retrieve
find out	discover	take off	remove (clothing); leave
get along	have friendly relations	take over	gain control of
get by	survive financially	throw away/out	put in the garbage
get over	recover	try on	wear something to see if it fits
get ready	prepare	turn off/on	stop/start a machine or light

EXERCISE 4

Underline the correct word in parentheses.

EXAMPLE: Please put (away / off) all of the files. Use the filing cabinet.

1. I am supposed to drop (out / in / off) a medical report at the lab, but now I can't find it. The file has been misplaced. Can you look (at / for / after) it? The file might be in the doctor's lounge. Please find (off / out / in) where it is. The last person who had the report did not put it (off / away / up). The file should have been put (into / on / about) the filing cabinet.

2. Martina is a receptionist and she earns minimum wage. She gets (on / by / out) financially, but sometimes she has to cut (off / back / away) on luxuries. For instance, she has cancelled her cable television subscription. The company where she works is losing money. Her boss has threatened to lay (out / off / on) another employee, so Martina is a little worried. She will put (out / away / off) her vacation to Spain until the workplace crisis passes. In the meantime, she will brush (up / off / at) on her Spanish.

The following sentences, which were written by students, have word-choice errors. Underline and correct each error.

EXAMPLE: Joquin is responsible <u>of</u> the cleaning. _____for_____

1. I have been a college student since many years. _____

2. I am not interested of science. _____

3. Every day, before I enter the lab, I must put a special coat and boots. _____

4. You should not throw off old cellular phones because they contain toxic components. _____

5. A social problem in our province is the school drop rate. _____

6. I have been working for the phone company since a long time. _____

7. At my job, I am responsible of many different projects. _____

8. People should give off smoking because it damages their lungs. _____

False Cognates

Cognates are words that look and sound alike in different languages and have the same meaning. For example, the English adjective *responsible* has the same meaning as the French or Spanish adjective *responsable*, although the words are spelled differently. **False cognates** are words that look like words in your language but do not have the same meaning.

Review this list of English words that students often misuse.

Term	Meaning	Example
animator	artist who makes animated movies or cartoons	Pixar hires talented **animators** to make children's cartoons.
group leader	team leader; coordinator	Annie is a **group leader** in a girls' camp.
host	moderator	Regis Philbin was the **host** of the game show *Who Wants to Be a Millionaire*.
actually	in fact; really	I thought I would like the concert, but I **actually** hated it.
currently	presently; right now	**Currently**, I am in the social sciences program.
deceived	misled; betrayed; lied to	My wife **deceived** me by dating another man.
disappointed	unhappy with results	I was **disappointed** when I failed the test.
stage	platform; period of growth	The actors performed on a **stage**. Children pass through **stages** of development.
scene	unit of action in a story; division or act of a play	We were nervous about the third **scene**. We filmed the love **scene** outdoors.
internship	training period	Stephan did an **internship** in an engineering firm.
experiment	scientific test or trial	The chemist conducted an **experiment** in his lab.
experience	event someone lives through	I had a difficult **experience** during my adolescence. ➡

Term	Meaning	Example
formation	structure or shape	We took photos of the glacial **formation**.
background	past experience	Karine has a **background** in sciences.
organism	living thing (plant, animal, or bacterium)	We examined the **organism** under a microscope.
organization	company or association	Ms. Chen works for a charitable **organization**.
doctor	medical practitioner	The injured patient went to a **doctor**.
medicine	drugs; medication	The patient was prescribed some **medicine**.

EXERCISE 6

Underline and correct one word-choice error in each sentence.

EXAMPLE: In your job, how much vacancy time do you get each year? *vacation*

1. We need someone to do an eight-week stage at our company. _____

2. I have a formation in accounting, and I believe that I could be a valuable asset to your team. _____

3. I would like to work for a vibrant non-profit organism. _____

4. In the past, I had a part-time job, but actually I am unemployed. _____

5. At my summer job in a children's camp, I was an animator for five-year-old children. _____

6. My ultimate career goal is to be either a pharmacist or a medicine. _____

7. Before I begin working full-time in a career, I want to travel to foreign lands and experiment life. _____

8. In your company, do you form new workers? _____

9. One day, I hope to play piano on a scene in front of an audience. _____

10. I felt quite deceived when the music conservatory didn't accept my application. _____

EXERCISE 7

Underline the appropriate word in parentheses.

1. When choosing a career, students should be (conscience / conscious) of its benefits and disadvantages. Electricians (accept / except) the risk of working on high-power wires. Acting, (witch / which / wich) seems like a great job, is very competitive. Actors undergo (through / though / thorough) training, and they must love being on a (scene / training / stage). The (principal / principle) reason to become an actor must be passion for the work. Also, actors should have a (formation / background) in literature.

2. Some students become (deceived / disappointed) because they cannot have the career of their choice. For instance, people with poor vision are not (aloud / allowed) to become airplane pilots. Also, experts do not (advice / advise) people with a fear of heights to become roofers. Someone with a fear of blood should not become a (medicine / doctor). Basically, a career choice must be a (personal / personnel) decision. If possible, students should get practical experience in a field. (Internships / Stages) are offered in many fields.

UNIT Review

Underline and correct ten word-choice errors.

1. Plastic garbage in oceans effects many fish species. It has been a problem since many years. I have a formation in political science, and I joined a political organism because I want to do something about the problem. I am responsible of educating people about plastic waste.

2. My political group depends of student helpers. We will hire some personal, including an animator to go on outings with some local students. The students will learn about the proper places to throw off garbage. I hope our project will success.

FINAL REVIEW

PART A

Underline the appropriate word in parentheses.

1. Sophia has wanted to become a police officer (since / for) a very long time. Her parents are not sure (weather / whether) or not Sophia is making the right decision. She depends (of / on) her parents to support her financially, so she has to consider their views. Her parents strongly (advice / advise) her to become a daycare teacher. However, Sophia can't (accept / except) their position and thinks that she should be (aloud / allowed) to make her own plans. She believes that her career choice must be a (personal / personnel) decision.

2. Sophia may take out a student loan. A lack of money will not (affect / effect) her decision. To help with living expenses, she plans to (sale / sell) her car. She also plans to cut (away / back / off) on luxuries and to live a simple life.

3. Sophia wants to specialize (in / on / at) domestic violence. She wants to help others, but that is not her (principal / principle) reason for joining a police force. Mainly, she hopes to have an exciting life. She is (conscience / conscious) that the work is dangerous, but she is not afraid (of / about) getting hurt. She has done (through / thorough / though) research, visited police stations, and met with officers.

PART B

Identify and correct five false cognates.

> *host*
> EXAMPLE: He asks the questions because he is the <u>animator</u> on a television quiz show.

4. When I was a child, I wanted to be a medicine, but actually I plan to become a writer. I'm not sure what type of formation a writer needs. I would love to work as a reporter at a large newspaper. Perhaps if I study journalism, I will be able to do a stage in a newspaper office. Last year, I submitted an article to our local newspaper. The article wasn't accepted, so I was quite deceived. Nonetheless, I will keep writing.

UNIT 4

WORD PARTS AND SPELLING

 Word Parts

A **root word** is the basic part of a word. A **prefix** is added to the beginning of a word. A **suffix** is added to the end of a word.

■ Prefixes, Scientific Roots, and Suffixes

Review the lists of common prefixes, root words, and suffixes.

Prefix		Root		Suffix	
alter-	other	adeno	gland	-agogue	leader
an-	without, lacking	bio	life	-ant -ent	connected with
ante-	before	carcin	cancer	-cide	killing
anti-	against	cardi	heart	-ic	relating to
bi-	two	cede	word	-ical	related to or consisting of
hyper-	over	commun	share	-ician	specialist
hypo-	under	derma	skin	-ism	practice of
inter-	between	emia	blood	-ist -ologist	one who adheres to a doctrine; specialist
mis-	wrong	hepato	liver	-itis	inflammation
mono-	one	neuro	nervous system	-logue	speech
omni-	all	onco/oma	tumour	-ology	study of
poly-	many	osteo	bone	-ous	quality or state
pre-	before	pater	father	-path	practitioner; one who suffers from a disease
proto-	first	pedo	child	-pathy	disease
re-	again	psych	mind	-phile	lover of
sub-	under	rhino	nose	-phone	sound
trans-	across	scient	knowing; skilful	-scope	examine
		socio	society	-ular	relating to

Break down each term into its parts to define it.

EXAMPLE: communist _one who adheres to the doctrine of sharing_

1. adenoma _____

2. dermatologist _____

3. osteopath _____

4. antecedent _____

5. cardiologist _____

6. patricide _____

7. anemia _____

8. rhinitis _____

9. carcinoma _____

10. omniscient _____

11. hepatitis _____

12. oncologist _____

■ Using Prefixes Meaning "Not"

The following prefixes mean "not."

il-   im-   in-   dis-   un-   non-   ir-

- Generally, use *il-* before words beginning with *l*.

    illogical   illegible

    Exceptions: ***dis**loyal*, ***un**likeable*

- Generally, use *im-* before words beginning with *m* or *p*.

    impossible   immobile

- Use *un-* before words beginning with *h*.

    unhappy   unhurt

    Note: The prefix *un-* can also appear before other letters: *unimportant*, *unlikeable*, etc.

EXERCISE **2**

Add a prefix meaning "not" to each word.

EXAMPLE: __un__ available

1. _____ -toxic

2. _____ legitimate

3. _____ polite

4. _____ interesting

5. _____ reliable

6. _____ patient

7. _____ harmed

8. _____ practical

9. _____ tolerant

10. _____ loyal

11. _____ appropriate

12. _____ friendly

■ Using Suffixes with Field-Related Terms

Be careful when writing the following field-related words.

Course or Program	Profession
biology	biologist
chemistry	chemist
economics	economist
physics	physicist
science	scientist
veterinary medicine	veterinarian

To turn these kinds of words into adjectives, you can often add *-al* or *-ic*.

-al: **biological** warefare   **chemical** imbalance   **political** choice

-ic: **scientific** test

EXERCISE 3

Change the nouns into adjectives by adding one of the suffixes from the list. You may need to remove or modify a letter.

-al	-able	-ical	-ary	-ic

EXAMPLE: mechanic*s* __al__

1. revolution_____
2. pessimist_____
3. athlete_____
4. environment_____

5. artist_____
6. sociology_____
7. politics_____
8. profit_____

9. biology_____
10. realist_____
11. nation_____
12. logic_____

TIP

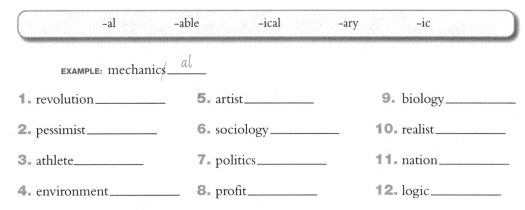

Confusing Words

Economic refers to the economy. *Economical* means cheap or inexpensive.

> The government will unveil its new **economic** policy.
> The most **economical** way to visit New York is by train.

Classic means first class, important, or masterful. *Classical* means "traditional" or "from the eighteenth to nineteenth centuries."

> The new Cohen brothers' movie will become an instant **classic**.
> I enjoy **classical** music such as the symphonies by Beethoven or Haydn.

EXERCISE 4

The following sentences, which appeared in students' writing, contain prefix or suffix errors. Underline and correct the errors.

EXAMPLE: I am not a *logical* logic thinker.

1. Last semester, I really enjoyed my economical and math classes.

2. My greatest weakness is that sometimes I am a nonreliable person.

3. Katherine is a patient, enthusiasm person, and she is studying to become a biochemical.

4. Marco is a realist person who enjoys physical and chemistry.

5. Melissa hopes to be a musician because she is very artistical and creative.

6. My dream is to become a veterinary because I have a deep love of animals and I can be diplomat with customers.

7. In the past, some nations engaged in biologic warfare.

8. Our prime minister should focus on long-term economical growth.

9. The most economic solution is to buy fresh fruits and vegetables.

Spelling Rules

Review these spelling rules to help yourself become a better speller.

■ Adding Suffixes

Words Ending in *e*

- Generally, when you add a suffix beginning with a vowel to a word ending in *e*, you drop the final *e*.

     noti**ce** ➡ noti**cing**   sen**se** ➡ sen**sible**   creati**ve** ➡ creati**vity**

   Exceptions: notic**eable**, chang**eable**, manag**eable**

- When you add a suffix beginning with a consonant to a word ending in *e*, keep the final *e*.

     definite ➡ definit**ely**   measure ➡ measur**em**ent   sure ➡ sur**ely**

Words Ending in *y*

- When you add an *-es* or *-ed* suffix to a word ending in a consonant + *y*, change the *y* to *i*.

     rely ➡ rel**ies**   study ➡ stud**ied**

- For words ending in a vowel + *y*, keep the *y*.

     stay ➡ sta**ys**   play ➡ pla**yed**

- When you add an *-ing* suffix, always keep the final *y*.

     rely ➡ rel**ying**   play ➡ pla**ying**   study ➡ stud**ying**

Words Ending in *ful*

Although the word *full* ends in two *l*'s, when *full* is added to another word as a suffix, it ends in one *l*. However, notice the unusual spelling when *full* and *fill* are combined: *fulfill*

     care**ful**   success**ful**   hope**ful**

■ Doubling the Final Consonant

Review the rules for doubling the final consonant of a root word.

- **One syllable words:** Double the final consonant of one-syllable words ending in a consonant-vowel-consonant pattern.

    rob ➜ ro**bb**er   hot ➜ ho**tt**est   zip ➜ zi**pp**ed

    Exceptions: root words ending in *w*, *x*, or *y*, such as *snowed*, *fixed*, or *joyous*

- **Words of two or more syllables:** Double the final consonant of words ending in a **stressed** consonant-vowel-consonant pattern.

    pre<u>fer</u> ➜ preferred   re<u>fer</u> ➜ referred   re<u>gret</u> ➜ regrettable

- If the last syllable is **not stressed**, then **do not double** the last letter of the word.

    <u>hap</u>pen ➜ happened   <u>vis</u>it ➜ visiting   <u>of</u>fer ➜ offered

Do not double the final consonant if the root word ends in a vowel and two consonants or if it ends with two vowels and a consonant.

    bias ➜ bia**s**ed   absorb ➜ absor**b**ed   mention ➜ mentio**n**ed

---

TIP

More on Double Letters

When the last letter of a prefix is the same as the first letter of the root word, you will have a double letter. For example, if you join *un-* and *natural*, the new word has a double *n* (*unnatural*). A similar rule applies to suffixes. For instance, if you add the suffix *–ly* to a word ending in *l*, the new word will have two *l*'s (*traditionally*).

Adding a prefix:	il + logical = illogical	over + ripe = overripe
Adding a suffix:	final + ly = finally	actual + ly = actually

EXERCISE 5

Write "C" next to correctly spelled words. If the word is incorrect, write the correct word in the blank.

EXAMPLE: usualy ___*usually*___   careful ___C___

1. ilegal _____
2. mispell _____
3. immoral _____
4. fullfill _____
5. helpfull _____
6. fataly _____
7. definitly _____
8. developped _____

9. regretable _____
10. iregular _____
11. openning _____
12. beginner _____
13. mentionned _____
14. awfuly _____
15. beautifull _____
16. noticeable _____

■ More Spelling Rules

• **Words ending in *gn*:** In words with a *gn* ending, the *g* is silent. Do not confuse them with words ending in *ng* such as *sing*.

>   si**gn**   ben**ign**   res**ign**

• **Words ending in *ght*, *th*, or *gh*:** The past forms of many verbs end in *ght*. In such words, the *gh* is silent and only the final *t* is pronounced. When saying words ending in *gth*, pronounce the final *th*.

>   bou**ght**   cau**ght**   BUT   len**gth**   wi**dth**

Some words end in *gh*. In such words, the final *gh* may be silent or it may have an *f* sound.

>   Silent *gh*:   thou**gh** bou**gh**
>   *gh* sounds like *f*:   lau**gh**   enou**gh**

• **Words with *ie* or *ei*:** Write *i* before *e*, except after *c* or when *ei* is pronounced as *ay*, as in *neighbour* and *weigh*.

>   bel**ie**ve   fr**ie**nd   ach**ie**ve   th**ie**f   p**ie**ce   perc**ei**ve   b**ei**ge

Exceptions: prot**ei**n   sc**ie**nce   h**ei**ght   eff**ic**ient   **ei**ther   n**ei**ther
                     for**ei**gner   l**ei**sure   soc**ie**ty   s**ei**ze   th**ei**r   w**ei**rd

Commonly Misspelled Words

Review this list of words that are commonly misspelled.

absence	desperate	harassment	privilege
accommodate	developed	interesting	professor
acquaintance	dilemma	laboratory	recommend
address	disappoint	leisure	responsible
alumni	embarrass	license	restaurant
appointment	encouragement	medicine	rhythm
approximate	engineer	mischievous	schedule
argument	environment	necessary	scientific
athlete	exaggerate	ninety	succeed
business	exercise	occasion	technique
campaign	extraordinarily	outrageous	thorough
committee	family	personality	tomorrow
conscience	future	possess	vacuum
conscientious	government	prejudice	wreckage

EXERCISE 6

Underline the correctly spelled word in each pair.

>   **EXAMPLE:** adress   <u>address</u>

1. future   futur   **6.** schedule   skedual

2. recommand   recommend   **7.** strenght   strength

3. exaggerate   exagerrate   **8.** taught   taugth

4. interresting   interesting   **9.** responsibility   responsability

5. laught   laughed   **10.** technic   technique

11. priviledge	privilege	16. engineer	ingeneer
12. familly	family	17. suceed	succeed
13. enought	enough	18. receive	recieve
14. government	governement	19. prejudice	predjudice
15. medecine	medicine	20. personnality	personality

TIP

One Word or Two?

A lot is always written as two words. However, the following are always written as one word.

another   cannot   everybody   anything

Be careful with the following, which can be written as one or two words.

already = before now   all ready = completely ready
everyday = ordinary; common   every day = each day
sometimes = occasionally   some time = at an eventual time

EXERCICE 7

Underline and correct sixteen spelling mistakes.

EXAMPLE: The parents reacted <u>angryly</u> when they were convicted.
angrily

1. At the moment, I am studing because I have to do alot of work in my program.

   I am already for my test tomorrow. In the futur, I plan to major in biologie because

   I am very interrested in that field. My goal is to become a medical lab technicien.

   Very few students are admited into the program, and it is very competitive. Last year,

   some students singed a petition asking the university to expand the program.

2. If I am accepted, I hope that I won't be disapointed. According to my profesor,

   there are a lot of job opportunities in this field. For example, many dental and

   medical supply buisnesses need people who can work in a labratory.

3. Sometime I feel discouraged. However, if I am not accepted into the science

   program, I have an other plan. I could study to become an ingeneer.

Answer the following questions. If necessary, go back and review the appropriate section.

1. Write down five prefixes that mean "not."

_____ _____ _____ _____ _____

2. Add *-ed* to the following verbs.

a) study _____ **d)** plan _____

b) open _____ **e)** offer _____

c) prefer _____ **f)** happen _____

3. Underline and correct spelling mistakes or prefix/suffix mistakes.

a) Doctors are usualy very carefull when they examine patients.

b) Boris laught when the governement minister made a mistake.

c) It is unecessary to worry about your skedule.

d) Frank's most artistical period was during his twenties.

e) The new minister must make very tough politic decisions.

f) I am normally an optimist person, so I see the good sides of situations.

FINAL REVIEW

PART A

Write "C" next to correctly written words. If the word is spelled incorrectly or if it has the wrong prefix, write the correct word in the blank.

EXAMPLES: regretable ____*regrettable*____ careful ____*C*____

1. fortunatly _____ **6.** preferes _____

2. unpatient _____ **7.** sincerly _____

3. normaly _____ **8.** studying _____

4. illegal _____ **9.** unatural _____

5. usefull _____ **10.** questionned _____

PART B

Underline and correct fifteen spelling errors.

applied
EXAMPLE: Jackson applyed for a nursing position.

11. In the futur, if you want a secure job, experts

recommend that you consider working in a health-

related field. You can become a lab technicien,

a doctor, or a radiologist. Also remember that there

is an acute nursing shortage. It is no exagerration

to say that nursing is one of the most important

proffesions in our society.

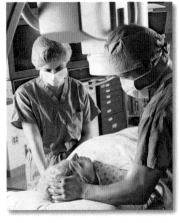

12. Nurses have diverse responsabilities. They give medecine to patients, and they

ensure that patients do not suffer from unecessary pain. Nurses must have a well-

developped personnality. They need to be compassionate when they communicate

with a patient and his or her familly. Of course, nurses must be in excellent health.

They need physical strenght because they may have to lift and move patients.

Nurses must also have a background in anatomy and biologie. In Canada, nurses

are paid by the governement. If you want to be succesful, please consider nursing.

PART C

Identify and correct a prefix or suffix error in each sentence. Write "C" next to correct
sentences.

diplomatic
EXAMPLE: I am very patient and diplomat.

13. There is a doctor shortage, so it is logic to train more medical students.

14. My decision to enter university next fall is not very realist.

15. I should try to become a veterinary instead because I am passionate about animals.

16. I will have to learn about diseases that are biological in origin.

17. I am not mechanical or artistical, but I am very scientific.

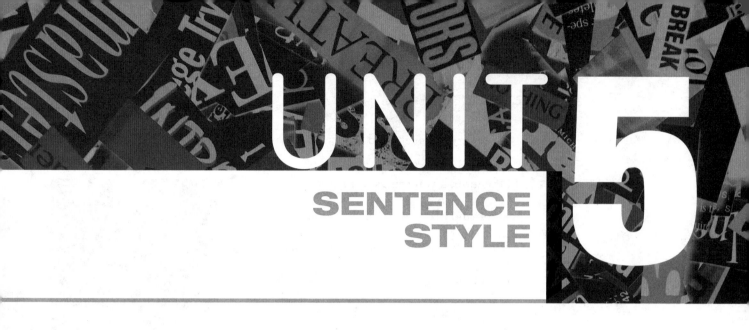

UNIT 5
SENTENCE STYLE

Complete Sentences

A sentence must express a complete idea. Review some key terms.

- A **phrase** is a group of words that is missing a subject, a verb, or both, and is not a complete sentence.

  on the weekend   without a doubt
  the best things in life   including metal pipes

- A **clause** is a group of words that contains a subject and a verb. There are two types of clauses. An **independent** or **main clause** stands alone and expresses one complete idea. An independent clause is also called a simple sentence.

  Welders wear specialized safety shoes and goggles.

  A **dependent** or **subordinate clause** has a subject and verb, but it cannot stand alone. It "depends" on another clause in order to be complete. A dependent clause usually begins with a subordinator such as *after, although, because, otherwise, unless,* or *when.* It can also begin with a relative pronoun such as *who, whom, which,* or *that.*

  because the work is dangerous
  which he has recommended

EXERCISE 1

Identify if the following are phrases or dependent clauses.

	Phrase	Clause
EXAMPLE: while we were working	_____	X
1. after we finish work	_____	_____
2. near the factory	_____	_____
3. which he did not ventilate	_____	_____
4. on September 12	_____	_____
5. although it is late	_____	_____
6. because they are exposed to flames	_____	_____

■ Avoiding Fragments and Run-ons

Ensure that your sentences have a subject and verb and express a complete idea. Avoid the following sentence errors.

Fragments

A fragment is an incomplete sentence. It may be missing a verb, main clause, or subject.

No verb:	First, the reasons to ban tasers.
No main clause:	Because the job requires it.
No subject:	And then drop out without realizing the consequences.

Run-ons

A run-on sentence occurs when two or more complete sentences are incorrectly connected either with a comma or no punctuation.

> Chemotherapy is effective, it kills cancer cells.

Run-on sentences can be corrected in various ways.

Make two sentences:	Chemotherapy is effective. **It** kills cancer cells.
Add a coordinator:	Chemotherapy is effective, **and** it kills cancer cells.
Add a subordinator:	Chemotherapy is effective **because** it kills cancer cells.
Add a semicolon:	Chemotherapy is effective; it kills cancer cells.

EXERCISE 2

Write "F" beside the fragments and "RO" beside the run-ons. Then correct each item.

EXAMPLES: Second, ^{accountants must enjoy} ^working with the public.   F

A survey was distributed ^^{, and} the results were analyzed.   RO

1. The two things I like in my program: chemistry and biology. _____

2. I'm good with numbers, that is why I enjoy math and science. _____

3. Most of the survey respondents were boys only thirty-five were girls. _____

4. Although there are serious side effects. _____

5. Working with the public is enjoyable, the job requires it. _____

6. For example, many students in each class. _____

7. Also, the problems with other types of plastics. _____

8. English skills are useful, many psychology books are in English. _____

9. Finally, the usefulness of math skills in my program. _____

10. One solution: rehabilitation instead of punishment. _____

11. Energy drink consumption is a big problem it affects a lot of people. _____

12. People do not save enough water, for example, they take long showers. _____

ⓐ Accurate Sentences

Some students make mistakes writing complex sentences. A **complex sentence** contains at least one main clause and one dependent clause (incomplete idea). Notice that the dependent clause can appear at the beginning, in the middle, or at the end of the sentence.

> **After Mr. Martin returns,** we will discuss the merger.
> The job offer **that I received** was fantastic.
> The company will close **because the executives mismanaged it**.

■ Using Subordinators

In complex sentences, dependent clauses often begin with a subordinator. Review the following list and ensure that you understand the meanings of the terms.

Cause or Reason	Condition or Result	Contrast	Place	Time
as	as long as	although	where	after
because	even if	even though	wherever	before
since	if	if		once
so that	only if	though		since
	provided that	whereas		until
	so that	unless		when
	unless			whenever
				while

If you use a subordinator at the beginning of a sentence, put a comma after the dependent clause. Generally, if you use a subordinator in the middle of the sentence, you do not need to use a comma.

> **Because** the alarm was ringing, the police arrived.
> The police arrived **because** the alarm was ringing.

EXERCISE 3

Fill in the blanks with an appropriate subordinator. Also add five missing commas.

EXAMPLE: ____*Because*____ he wants to be his own boss ⱽLeo became a plumber.

1. Most plumbers spend up to two years as apprentices _____ they

can hone their skills on the job. Simon Townshend became a plumber

_____ he loves working on construction projects. _____

he earns enough money he hopes to build his own house.

2. Plumbing requires various skills. _____ he calculates the lengths

of pipes Simon needs to understand math concepts. _____ he works

in tight places Simon needs to have dexterity.

3. _____ Simon occasionally works alone he usually works with a

master plumber. _____ plumbers are in demand Simon did not find

a job easily. These days, Simon travels _____ his job requires it.

■ Using Transitional Words and Expressions

A **transitional expression** can appear at the beginning of a sentence. It can also link
two complete ideas and show how they are related.

Addition	Alternative	Contrast	Time	Example or Emphasis	Result or Consequence
additionally	in fact	despite	eventually	for example	consequently
also	in spite of	however	finally	for instance	hence
besides	instead	nevertheless	later	namely	therefore
furthermore	on the contrary	nonetheless	meanwhile	of course	thus
in addition	on the other	still	next	undoubtedly ·	
moreover	hand		subsequently		
	otherwise				

A compound sentence is composed of two complete and independent ideas. You can
join the two ideas with a coordinating conjunction (*and, but, or, nor, yet*). Place a comma
before the coordinating conjunction. You can also join two sentences with a transitional
expression. Place a semicolon before the transition and a comma after it. As you review
the following sentences, notice how they are punctuated.

Simple:	The building is in terrible condition. However, it can be renovated.
Compound:	The building is in terrible condition, **but** it can be renovated.
	The building is in terrible condition; **however,** it can be renovated.
	The building is in terrible condition; **of course,** it can be renovated.

T I P

However and *Although*

Do not confuse *however* with *although*. *However* means "but in any case" and introduces a
contrast. *Although* is part of a dependent clause, and it means "even if." *Although*, *even though*,
and *though* mean the same thing. Notice how the sentences are punctuated.

Semicolon and comma:	The paint is very expensive; **however,** we should buy it.
Comma:	**Although** the paint is expensive, we should buy it.
No comma:	We should buy the paint **even though** it is expensive.

Underline the best word in parentheses. It may be a transitional expression or a subordinator.

> **EXAMPLE:** I want to build a house; (unless / <u>therefore</u>), I will need to hire some construction workers.

1. I am interested in building a house (while / even if) it is very expensive.

2. Many professionals must cooperate to build a structure; (therefore / otherwise), the building could have significant problems.

3. (Although / However) architects design buildings, engineers can also design large structures.

4. (Although / Because) the permit office is closed, I can't get my permit today.

5. (Although / In spite of) the warning from the engineer, the contractor used cement that was too thin.

6. The roofers refuse to change the rotten wood on my roof (unless / whereas) I offer them more money.

7. I will pay for the bricks with cash; (although / however), I will use my credit card to pay for the wood.

8. I love houses constructed of wood (whereas / so that) my father prefers houses made of concrete.

9. The walls are standing; (although, however), the roof still needs to be completed.

■ Avoiding Faulty Logic

Ensure that your sentences have a logical meaning. Use precise vocabulary.

> Incorrect: Dyslexia is **when** you cannot read easily.
> (Dyslexia is not a time.)
> Correct: Dyslexia is a learning disorder characterized by difficulty reading.

T I P

Because and *Because Of*

Because of is a phrasal preposition that means "due to." It appears before a noun or pronoun. *Because* is a conjunction that appears before a clause containing a subject and verb. Notice the differences in the following sentences.

Because of + noun phrase
Because of the rain, the roofers can't work today.
Because + clause
Because it is raining, the roofers can't work today.

When people speak informally, they may use *'cause* to mean *because*. However, do not use that shortcut in your writing.

>   **because**
> I quit my job ~~cause~~ the hours were too long.

The following sentences appeared in student writing. Add, modify, or remove words to make them more precise. There may be more than one way to correct each sentence.

EXAMPLE: Because $\overset{\text{of}}{\vee}$ the rain, we must work indoors.

1. A genius is when someone has an exceptional talent or intellect.

2. Networking is where you stay in contact with people to help your career.

3. Dylan is really happy cause he just received a job with a contractor.

4. He gets along well with others thought he is often moody.

5. Even you may want to change your past, you cannot.

6. Anorexia is where you have an eating disorder.

7. Daniel cannot become a pilot cause he has very poor eyesight.

8. Because the math requirement, I was not accepted into the pure sciences program.

■ Using Relative Pronouns

A relative pronoun describes a noun or pronoun. The most common relative pronouns are the following:

> that   which   who (whoever)   whom (whomever)   whose

That: Use *that* to add information about a **thing**.

> The stocks **that we bought** are now worthless.

Which: Use *which* to add **non-essential** information about a **thing**.

> The stock market**, which peaked in 2008,** has fallen in recent years.

Who: Use *who* (or *whoever*) to add information about a **person**. *Who* is followed by a verb.

> The woman **who built the cabinet** hurt herself.
> I will work with **whoever is the most efficient**.

Whom*: *Whom* is the objective form of *who* and replaces *him, her, them, me,* or *us.* Use *whom* to add information about a person. *Whom* is usually followed by a noun or pronoun.

> The builder needs to hire someone **whom he can trust**.
> He will hire **whomever you suggest**.

Whose: Use *whose* to show possession. *Whose* replaces *his, her, its,* or *their.*

> The person **whose house we're building** has gone bankrupt.

---

* *Whom* is used in formal contexts; people rarely use it when speaking. Some linguists believe that *whom* may disappear from the English language one day.

TIP

Using *That* or *Which*

Both *which* and *that* refer to things, but *which* refers to non-essential ideas. Also, *which* can imply that you are referring to the complete subject and not just a part of it. Compare the following two sentences. Notice that clauses with *which* are always set off with commas.

The bricks **that** are cracked need to be replaced.
(This sentence suggests that some of the bricks are not cracked.)

The bricks**, which** are cracked, need to be replaced.
(This sentence suggests that all of the bricks are cracked.)

EXERCISE **6**

Complete the sentences with *that, which, who, whom,* or *whose.*

EXAMPLE: People ___who___ repair computers must continually update their knowledge.

1. An article _____ I recently read described ten hot jobs in the computer field.

2. A person _____ cares about the environment could become an environment simulations developer.

3. He or she would create programs _____ predict the effects of global warming.

4. Environmental models, _____ are analyzed by professionals, will help governments make decisions.

5. Another job _____ sounds interesting is in video game development.

6. Video games are not just for people _____ want to play.

7. Health and education departments buy video games, _____ are available online, to help train employees.

8. A woman _____ I have recently met told me about the benefits of video games in therapy.

9. She described a boy _____ she had previously worked with.

10. The child, _____ was very shy, would not speak to the therapist.

11. The child's mother, _____ anger was evident, expected instant results.

12. A video game _____ had special segments helped the therapist make a diagnosis.

T I P

Easily Confused Words

Do not confuse the following terms. Review their meanings.

Than, Then, or That

Than is used to compare two things.   Alex is older **than** I am.
Then means "at a particular time."   She retired, and **then** she moved to France.
That introduces a clause.   The book **that** I read is very long.

Who's or Whose

Who's is the contracted form of *who is*.   We will hire someone **who's** efficient.
Whose indicates possession.   Is that the man **whose** wife left him?

EXERCISE 7

Underline and correct twelve errors in *who, whom, whose, which, then, than,* and *that.*
Look for incorrect or misspelled words.

1. One of the most dangerous occupations is high-rise construction work. It is much
more dangerous then most other construction jobs. For example, the workers which
built the Empire State Building had to walk on beams up to 102 storeys high.

2. In the past, high-rise builders, who's lives were at risk, had
no safety equipment. With bare heads and ordinary work
boots, they walked on the narrow beams. Today, hard hats
and safety harnesses, wich companies must provide, are
given to workers. However, an ironworker, who name is
Ben, says that the safety harnesses are cumbersome and
inconvenient. "When a beam is swinging on a wire and
coming toward me, I need to be able to move out of the way quickly. I can't always
do that when I'm wearing a harness."

3. Modern skyscrapers, who are made with steel frames, have to bear the weight of
hundreds of windows. Sometimes the engineers which design the buildings make
mistakes. For instance, the John Hancock Tower in Boston, who is covered with
mirrored glass, is not secure during high winds. Huge panels of glass than weigh up
to 225 kilograms (500 pounds) have fallen to the pavement. Montreal's new library
building has similar problems. In the summer of 2005, six of the decorative glass

panels fell to the sidewalk below. Luckily, pedestrians whom were in the vicinity were not injured.

4. These days, our city is planning to build a tower than will have over eighty floors. The construction company needs a project manager and will only hire someone whose qualified for the job.

Varied Sentences

A passage filled with simple short sentences can sound choppy. When you vary the lengths of your sentences, the same passage becomes easier to read and flows more smoothly. Also, when your sentences all begin with similar words, you risk boring your reader. An effective way to make your sentences more vivid is to vary the opening words.

To create varied sentences openings, you could try the following strategies.

- Begin with a **prepositional phrase**.

    On blogs and social networks, the company promotes its products.

- Begin with a **present participle** (word ending in –*ing*).

    Hoping to increase sales, the company offers incentives to managers.

- Begin with a **past participle**.

    Pleased with his team, the manager recited sales figures.

Now read the following two paragraphs. The first paragraph is choppy and repetitive. The second paragraph, which has varied sentence types and openings, flows better.

Simple Sentences
Zara is a successful Spanish fashion chain. **Zara** could become the world's largest clothing retailer, according to *BusinessWeek* magazine. **Zara** has over six hundred outlets. **Zara** may overtake the Gap. **Zara** has a very efficient supply chain. **Zara** reacts quickly to new fashions. **Zara** puts new designs on the market in as little as two weeks.

Varied Sentence Types and Varied Openings
Zara is a successful Spanish fashion chain. According to *BusinessWeek* magazine, Zara could become the world's largest retailer. The clothing retailer, which has over six hundred outlets, may overtake Gap. Reacting quickly to new fashions, Zara has a very efficient supply chain. In as little as two weeks, the company puts new designs on the market.

EXERCISE **8**

Combine the pairs of sentences using a variety of methods. You may need to delete, add, or rearrange words.

EXAMPLE: Welding can be dangerous. Kelly enjoys it.

Although welding can be dangerous, Kelly enjoys it.

1. The welder lives in Vancouver. She is a woman.

2. Kelly Bruce does welding. It is quite dangerous.

_____

3. She competed for a position at an aircraft company. She got the job.

_____

4. She excels at aluminum welding. She does very detailed work.

_____

5. Kelly wears a face shield. The shield protects her eyes from sparks.

_____

6. Welders work in well-ventilated areas. They must limit their exposure to fumes.

_____

7. Kelly is very strong. She must lift heavy pipes.

_____

8. Welders are well-paid for their work. Welders have an important job.

_____

T I P

Using Appositives

Another way to combine ideas and provide variety is to add appositives to your sentences.
An **appositive** is a word or phrase that gives further information about a noun or pronoun.
You can place the appositive directly before the word that it refers to or directly after that word.
Notice that the appositives are set off with commas.

> **A single mother,** Alexis Reed repairs electric wires.
> Alexis Reed, **a single mother,** repairs electric wires.

EXERCISE 9

Edit the following paragraph so that the opening words are varied. Also, combine some
sentences to create variety.

> Cynthia Cook is an ironworker. She is the mother of two children. She is originally
> from Quebec. She is a female in a male-dominated field. She was hired at the age of
> twenty-two. She started her first job at a nuclear power plant. She picked up skills
> quickly. Her job is rewarding. It has good pay and benefits. She feels safe on high beams
> these days.

_____

_____

_____

_____

_____

_____

_____

_____

_____

UNIT Review

Think about what you have learned in this unit. If you do not know an answer, then go back and review that section.

Identify and correct errors in fragments, run-ons, punctuation, or sentence logic.

1. Second, the disadvantages of private clinics.

2. Patients will go to private clinics, it could relieve the public system.

3. Some people cannot afford to pay, a private health-care system is not fair

for the poor.

4. I want a public health system even I have to wait for treatment.

5. Chemotherapy is when a person gets treated for cancer.

6. I work with the public. Because my job requires it.

FINAL REVIEW

PART A

Complete the sentences. Circle the letters of the appropriate answers.

1. Michael Resnick became a welder ... the good pay and benefits.

   a) due   **b)** because   **c)** because of   **d)** after

2. Resnick bought a Type 1 arc welder, ... is expensive, because he wants to create metal sculptures.

   a) that   **b)** who   **c)** what   **d)** which

3. Resnick's sister, ... house he lives in, is helping him buy the welder.

a) who's   b) whose   c) whom   d) who

4. Chantal Resnick is a woman ... you have never met.

a) whom   b) which   c) whose   d) who's

5. ... the poor condition of his tools, Mike uses them regularly.

a) Although   b) Despite   c) Because   d) Since

6. ... he cannot speak German, he was hired to work with German clients.

a) Because   b) Despite   c) Although   d) Althought

7. Most of his sculptures are large; ..., his bird sculpture is just six inches tall.

a) however   b) although   c) because   d) even

8. ... he is not very talented, his sculptures sell well.

a) Even   b) In spite of   c) Unless   d) Even though

9. These days, Michael Resnick has about fifty sculptures ... are in his garage.

a) who   b) what   c) wich   d) that

10. He plans to weld a new sculpture ... represents freedom.

a) than   b) that   c) who   d) what

PART B

Edit the following sentences for run-on, fragment, or logic errors. Write "C" next to correct sentences.

EXAMPLE:

My program is very popular, it is difficult to get accepted into it.

11. Two things I love in my program: the labs and the other students.

12. The chemistry labs, who are difficult, teach me many things.

13. I need English because the American clients.

14. I don't like philosophy although, I think it could be useful for my personal growth.

15. I have mathematical skills, that is why I like my physics course.

UNIT 6

QUOTING, PARAPHRASING, AND SUMMARIZING

To incorporate the results of your research into your writing, you can quote, paraphrase, or summarize the original material. In all three cases, you must cite the original source.

- When you **quote**, you either directly state a person's exact words (with quotation marks) or report them (without quotation marks).

- When you **paraphrase**, you use your own words to present someone's ideas. A paraphrase is close to the same number of words as the original selection.

- When you **summarize**, you use your own words to briefly state the main ideas of another work. A summary is much shorter than the original selection.

a Quoting Sources

Quotations can reveal the opinions of an expert or highlight ideas that are particularly memorable and important. A **direct quotation** contains the exact words of an author, and the quotation is set off with quotation marks.

> The police officer said, "White-collar crime is increasing."

To learn how to introduce or integrate quotations in your writing, read the following original selection and then read about three common methods. The examples in this unit follow the citation methods recommended in the *MLA Handbook for Writers of Research Papers*, the most popular standard in North American schools.

Original Selection

Sanitation has been a triumph of modern medicine, all but eradicating many diseases and parasites. We've whipped the body louse, trichinosis, typhoid, and childbed fever, and we're not a bit nostalgic. But there are signs that this very preoccupation with good hygiene is making some of us sick. Many immune system disorders are on the rise.

> McCarthy, Susan. "Talking Dirty." *Salon*.
> Salon Media Group. 3 May 2000. Web.

1. Phrase

Introductory phrase: Introduce the quotation with a phrase followed by a comma. Capitalize the first word in the quotation.

> In her *Salon* article, "Talking Dirty," Susan McCarthy writes, **"M**any immune system disorders are on the rise.**"**

Interrupting phrase: Another approach is to start a sentence with the beginning of the quote and then interrupt it to indicate who is being quoted. Place the comma after the first part of the quotation, and place another comma after the interrupting phrase.

> "Sanitation," writes McCarthy, "has been a triumph of modern medicine, all but eradicating many diseases and parasites."

End phrase: Give the complete quote and place the phrase citing the source after the quotation. End the quotation with a comma instead of a period.

> "But there are signs that this preoccupation with good hygiene is making some of us sick," writes Susan McCarthy.

If your quotation ends with other punctuation, put it inside the quotation mark.

> "What are the costs?" the student asked.
> "That question cannot be answered!" the officer replied.

2. Sentence

With this method, you introduce the quotation with a sentence followed by a colon. Capitalize the first word in the quotation.

> McCarthy suggests that there are consequences to our preoccupation with cleanliness: "Many immune system disorders are on the rise."

3. Integrated Quotation

If the quotation is integrated into your sentence, place quotation marks around the source's exact words. Do not capitalize the first word in the quotation.

> According to McCarthy, over-emphasis on cleanliness "is making some of us sick" and can lead to asthma and other ailments.

4. Inside Quotation

If one quotation is inside another quotation, then use single quotation marks (' ') around the inside quotation.

> The officer said, "The perpetrator confronted me and shouted, 'Do you know who I am?'"

TIP

Page Numbers

If your quotation is from a print source such as a book, newspaper, or magazine, put the page number in parentheses. Put the final period after the page number.

> In his book *Criminal Justice*, John Fuller writes, "Elder citizens demonstrate the greatest fear of street crime, yet they are the least likely to encounter it" **(11).**

EXERCISE 1

In the following sentences, the quotations are blue. Punctuate each sentence. Add commas, periods, colons, and capital letters where necessary. Note that the number in parentheses indicates the page number of the book or magazine from which the quote was taken.

EXAMPLE: Victor Borge said Laughter is the closest distance between two people

1. According to Fuller, police officers must confront the issue of street people arresting

a vagrant who has harmed nobody may seem unjust (24)

2. G. Gordon Liddy says obviously crime pays, or there would be no crime

3. The criminal yelled I'm innocent but criminals all say that reported Detective Hussein

4. Forensic nurses support the legal system says Ronald G. Burns by dealing with assault victims and dangerous offenders (56)

5. Behind every great fortune, there is a crime wrote Honoré de Balzac

6. Timothy Lynch asks so what exactly is plea bargaining

7. The detective said that crime scene evidence must be analyzed by professionals

8. Evidence is anything that might assist a court of law says Wilson Sullivan (2)

■ Using Ellipses (...)

Use ellipsis marks (...) to show that you have omitted unnecessary information from a quotation. When you type the three periods, leave a space before and after each period. Do not put parentheses or brackets around the three dots.

If you remove the last part of a sentence, you can insert the three spaced periods and then a final period to signal the end of the sentence, as shown below.

> According to Susan McCarthy, "Sanitation has been a triumph of modern medicine, all but eradicating many diseases and parasites. . . . But there are signs that this very preoccupation with good hygiene is making some of us sick."

■ Using Brackets

Use square brackets to make a correction or an insertion into a quoted extract. If a quotation contains a spelling mistake, put *[sic]* in brackets after the error.

Use brackets to show missing information.

> "If not for my lawyer **[Ian Willing]**, I would still be in prison," said Rowlands.

Use brackets to indicate a spelling error.

> The convict wrote, "I'm inocent **[sic]** and I will prove it."

EXERCISE **2**

Practise integrating quotations. Read the following selection and then make different types of quotations. The selection appeared on page 15 of Wilson T. Sullivan's book, *Crime Scene Analysis*.

> Glass provides valuable evidence. When you observe glass in a fire scene, determine if the soot is baked on. If so, it was most likely a slow-moving fire. If the soot is readily wiped off the glass, then you have a fast-moving fire and should look for an accelerant.

1. Introduce your quotation with a phrase.

_____

_____

_____

2. Introduce your quotation with a sentence.

_____

_____

_____

3. Interrupt your quotation with a phrase.

_____

_____

_____

4. Include ellipses in your quotation.

_____

_____

_____

EXERCISE **3**

Identify and correct the errors in each of the following quotations.

EXAMPLE: Dorothy Parker said ,"I don't care what is written about me".

1. Sullivan writes: "A broken window at a fire scene may imply that someone broke into the building." (135)

2. "Glass provides valuable evidence." says Sullivan (135). "

3. "Boxing", says Frank Bruno, "is just show business with blood".

4. Einstein described the importance of creative thinking, "imagination is more important than knowledge."

5. In _Technical Communication_, Lannon states: "Gossip, personal messages, and complaints about the boss all might be read by unintended receivers (484). "

6. Crime victim Alex Baya explained what happened "The thief yelled, "I will find

you!" as he left the building."

Writing Titles

Capitalize the major words in titles. It is not necessary to capitalize articles (*a, an, the*), conjunctions (*and, but, or*), or prepositions (*in, on, of,* etc.) unless they are the first or last word of the title. Please note that all verbs and pronouns should be capitalized, even if they are short words such as *is* or *it*.

Place the title of a short work in quotation marks. Italicize (or underline if you are handwriting a document) the title of a longer document.

Short Works		Long Works	
Web article:	"Child Care"	Website:	*Statistics Canada*
Newspaper article:	"Economic Crisis Deepens"	Newspaper:	*The Globe and Mail*
Magazine article:	"New Artists"	Magazine:	*Rolling Stone*
Essay:	"Hip-Hop Nation"	Textbook:	*Common Culture*
Short story:	"The Awakening"	Book:	*The Catcher in the Rye*
TV episode:	"The Lie"	TV series:	*Lost*
Song:	"Mouths to Feed"	CD:	*Release Therapy*
		Movie:	*Donnie Darko*
		Artwork:	*Sunflowers*

EXERCISE **4**

Set off ten titles and add five missing capital letters. Add quotation marks to the titles of short works. For long works, underline titles that should be in italics.

EXAMPLE: The magazine r̲olling s̲tone featured successful singers.
                         R   S

1. The song Mad World was first recorded by the British band Tears for Fears. Released

in 1982 as a single and the following year on the album The hurting, the song was

moderately successful. Then, for the 2001 movie Donnie Darko, the song was

re-recorded in a slower tempo with piano music. That version, by Gary Jules and

Michael Andrews, mesmerized filmgoers and helped give the movie a cult following.

The song has appeared as background music in television shows such as Third Watch

and Without a trace. Then, in 2009, Adam Lambert sang it during an episode

of American Idol. Once again, the song became a great hit.

2. The music magazine Rolling stone has an article on its website called The RS 500 Greatest Songs of All Time. The first item on the list is Bob Dylan's song Like a rolling Stone. According to the magazine, the greatest album is Sgt. Pepper's Lonely Hearts Club band.

Paraphrasing and Summarizing

When you paraphrase or summarize, you restate someone's ideas using your own words. The main difference between a paraphrase and a summary is the length. While a paraphrase can be the same length as the original selection, a summary is much shorter.

■ How to Paraphrase

To paraphrase, do the following:

- Highlight the main ideas in the original text.
- Restate the main ideas using your own words. You can keep specialized words, common words, and names of people or places. However, find synonyms for other words and use your own sentence structure.
- Use a dictionary or thesaurus, if necessary, to find synonyms.
- Maintain the original author's ideas and intent.
- Do not include your own opinions.
- After you finish writing, proofread your text.
- Acknowledge the author and title of the original text.

Remember that a paraphrase is roughly the same length as the original selection.

Original Selection

Quebec's capital, incidentally, is another safe haven. Its crime score for the six offences tracked in the *Maclean's* index (murder, robbery, aggravated assault, sexual assault, breaking and entering, and auto theft) ranked 40 percent below the national average in 2007. . . . Even more impressive for a city of 535,000, it recorded not a single homicide that year—by far the largest of thirty-four cities that were murder-free.

MacQueen, Ken. "The Rankings: Canada's Most Dangerous Cities." *Maclean's*. 5 March, 2009. Web.

Paraphrase

Quebec City, with its population of just over half a million, is a relatively secure place to live, according to a *Maclean's* report. For example, in 2007, there were no murders in Quebec City, which is remarkable considering the city is among the largest cities in the study to have no homicides. Also, in 2007, that city's crime rate for theft, rape, and other crimes was less than half the Canadian average.

■ How to Summarize

When you summarize, you condense a message to its basic elements. Do the following:

- Read the original text carefully because you will need a complete picture before you begin to write.

- Ask yourself *who*, *what*, *when*, *where*, *why*, and *how* questions to help you identify the central ideas of the text.
- Reread your summary. Ensure that you have expressed the essential message in your own words.
- Your summary should be a maximum of 30 percent of the original length.
- Cite the original source.

In written summaries, readers should be able to understand the essential message. The complete document would contain details and examples, but readers would not require the original to make sense of the central ideas.

Here is a summary of the selection used in the previous example:

According to a *MacLean's* report, Quebec City is a secure place to live, with a crime rate that is much lower than the Canadian average.

EXERCISE 5

Paraphrase and summarize the following selections.

1. Young men were less likely to be engaged in school than young women and were more likely to report wanting to work/earn money as a reason for dropping out of high school. In contrast, teenage pregnancy plays a larger role in the decision to drop out of high school for young women. According to the Youth in Transition Survey, 15.9 percent of female drop-outs left school because they were pregnant or because they needed to tend to their child.

Bowlby, Geoff. "Provincial Drop-out Rates: Trends and Consequences." *Education Matters.* Statistics Canada. 2005. Web.

Paraphrase: _____

_____

_____

_____

_____

_____

Summary: _____

_____

_____

2. Unfortunately it turns out that hit men, genocidal maniacs, gang leaders, and violent kids often have high self-esteem, not low self-esteem. A recipe for their violence is a mean streak combined with an unwarranted sense of self-worth. When such a boy comes across a girl or parents or schoolmates who communicate to him that he is not all that worthy, he lashes out.

Seligman, Martin. "The American Way of Blame." APA Monitor Online. *American Psychological Association.* July 1998. Web.

Paraphrase: _____

_____

_____

Summary: _____

_____

_____

Answer the following questions. If necessary, go back and review the appropriate section.

1. What is the difference between a summary and a paraphrase?

_____

_____

2. When you introduce a quotation with a phrase, what should you place before the quotation marks?

a) comma   **b)** colon

3. When you introduce a quotation with a complete sentence, what should you place before the quotation marks?

a) comma   **b)** colon

4. Punctuate the following quotations. The exact quotation is in blue.

a) Macdonald said The pesticides are causing the collapse of bee colonies .

b) Macdonald blames pesticides for the death of bees They are getting disoriented .

c) The pesticides are causing the collapse of bee colonies said Macdonald .

d) According to Macdonald Ellen Parks said Look what is happening to the bees !

PART **A**

Circle the letter of the correct answer.

1. The article, called ..., discusses the problems off the coast of Somalia.

   a) *Pirate battles*   **b)** *Pirate Battles*   **c)** "Pirate battles"   **d)** "Pirate Battles"

2. The CBC journalist stated ... Somali pirates were initially motivated by anger ...

   a) :" / ".   **b)** ," / ."   **c)** :" / ."   **d)** ," / ".

3. "Western nations ... he said ... had been dumping toxic containers off the Somali coast for decades."

   a) :" / .".   **b)** ", / ,"   **c)** " / ,"   **d)** ," / ,"

4. The old man spoke of the past ... We could fish off this coast ...

   a) :" / " (6).   **b)** ," / ." (6)   **c)** :" / ." (6)   **d)** ," / " (6).

5. The essay ... appears on the website ...

   a) "Bee deaths" / "Salon."   **b)** *Bee Deaths* / "Salon."   **c)** "Bee Deaths" / *Salon.*

PART **B**

Read the following selection. Then write a paraphrase and a summary.

1. A county government in central China has rescinded an order which was intended to make officials smoke more to help the local economy, local authorities said on Tuesday. Functionaries in Gongan county in rural Hubei province had been ordered to smoke at least 23,000 packs of cigarettes a year, worth nearly 4 million yuan ($586,700), to cushion government finances, according to regional media reports. Those who failed to meet smoking targets or were caught smoking brands from other provinces would have been fined, the reports added, citing a government document issued earlier this year.

> "China Cigarette Order Goes up in Smoke." *Reuters.*
> Reuters.com. 5 May 2009. Web.

Paraphrase: _____

_____

_____

_____

_____

_____

Summary: _____

_____

_____

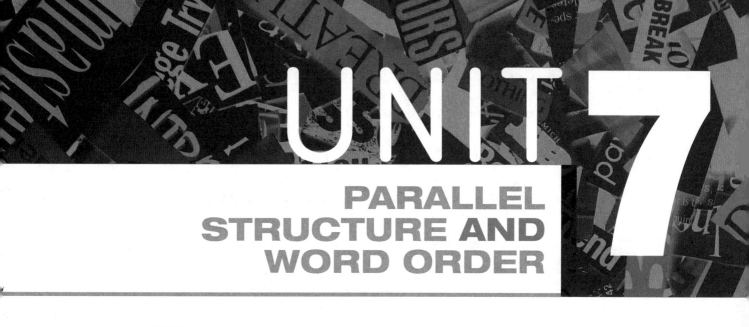

UNIT 7

PARALLEL STRUCTURE AND WORD ORDER

a Parallel Structure

■ Faulty Parallel Structure

Pairs or groups of items in a sentence should have a balanced grammatical structure. **Faulty parallel structure** occurs when verbs, phrases, or clauses are not balanced.

Not parallel: **Biology**, **chemistry**, and the study of physics are his favourite courses.

Parallel nouns: **Biology**, **chemistry**, and **physics** are his favourite courses.

Not parallel: We find news **in newspapers**, **on television**, and by looking on the Internet.

Parallel phrases: We find news **in newspapers**, **on television**, and **on the Internet**.

Not parallel: Ms. Roy will hire someone **who is educated**, has experience, and **who wants a challenge**.

Parallel clauses: Ms. Roy will hire someone **who is educated**, **who has experience**, and **who wants a challenge**.

EXERCISE **1**

The following sentences appeared in student writing samples. Underline and correct errors involving parallel structure.

EXAMPLE: In my yoga courses, I learned to anticipate and ~~dealing~~ *deal* with stress.

1. She hates reading books, writing dissertations, and she hates big projects. *doing*

2. He dislikes the boring teachers he has to listen to, the huge projects he has to do, and sociology. *The class he has to study.*

3. His strengths are his patience, his good communication skills, and ~~he is a good listener.~~ *his good listening skills.*

4. He likes his program because of the skills he learns, the people he meets, and

~~he really likes~~ the play he acts in.

                                        her social skills and her organization
5. Her strengths are her logic, ~~she's a people person,~~ ~~and~~ organization.

                        as
6. I have experience as a cashier, a waitress, and ~~I was working~~ as a store clerk.

                                                            challenging
7. The electrical technology program is stimulating and ~~a challenge~~.

                                                    his reliable
8. He is known for his integrity, his creativity, and ~~he's dependable~~.

                        graphic designers
9. Some painters, sculptors, and ~~people who do graphic~~ design give courses in our college.

EXERCISE 2

The following résumé contains errors typically found in student writing. Underline and correct nine examples of faulty parallel structure. Look in sentences, but also look at lists.

Kiera Moreau
25 Lyon Boulevard
Toronto, ON M5M 3C2

OBJECTIVE Position as an assistant manager

                        Graduated
EDUCATION **Diploma in Business Management**, June 2008
            Seneca College, Toronto, Ontario

EMPLOYMENT **Cashier and Server**   from
            MC Café, Queen Street   January 2008 ~~to present~~

- Prepare food and drinks

- Working with the public

- Handling cash and compiled receipts

Nursing Home Worker
Well Springs, Yonge Street   Summer 2007

- Dealing with people with diverse needs

- Good customer service

- Negotiated with food service workers

- Communicating with seniors

- I had to clean the dining room area

SKILLS	I am fluent in English and French
	Familiar with Adobe Photoshop and Microsoft Office
ACTIVITIES	I am a volunteer at a refugee centre
	Coach a basketball team

■ Parallel Structure in Comparisons

Use parallel structure in comparisons containing *than* or *as*.

Not parallel:	**Designing** a sculpture is easier than <u>to</u> actually <u>sculpt</u> it.
Parallel *-ing* forms:	**Designing** a sculpture is easier than actually **sculpting** it.
Not parallel:	**Art** is as important as <u>the work of a mathematician</u>.
Parallel nouns:	**Art** is as important as **mathematics**. OR
	The work of an artist is as important as **the work of a mathematician**.

■ Parallel Structure in Two-Part Constructions

Use parallel structure for the following paired items.

either … or ✓	not … but ✓	both … and ⌣
neither … nor ✓	not only … but also ✓	rather … than ⌣

Not parallel:	I find the painting neither **interesting** nor <u>is it a work of beauty</u>.
Parallel adjectives:	I find the painting neither **interesting** nor **beautiful**.
Not parallel:	Not only **the retailers** but <u>the people who shop there</u> are also angry about the price increases.
Parallel nouns:	Not only **the retailers** (but) also **the customers** are angry about the price increases.

TIP

Using *Either … or* and *Neither … Nor*

When joining two independent clauses with *either … or* or *neither … nor*, ensure that your sentence is properly structured. *Neither* or *either* must appear before the first item in the pair, not after it.

neither in an office nor outdoors
My ideal workplace is **not** ~~in an office, but~~ **neither** ~~outdoors~~.

EXERCISE 3

The following sentences appeared in student papers. Underline and correct errors in parallel structure or the placement of *neither* or *either*.

neither hard working nor lazy.

EXAMPLE: I am not hard working neither I am lazy.

has not only mechanical skills but also artistic skills

1. My father <u>has both mechanical skills and skills as an artist.</u>

2. My father would rather build furniture than <u>being an accountant.</u>

count numbers.

I rather write a story than read one.

3. For me, writing a story is more entertaining than to read one.

I am neither my father nor my mother.

4. I am not like my father neither like my mother.

hard work

5. In my field, intelligence is as important as ~~working hard.~~

my friends

6. Not only my co-workers but also ~~the people I am friends with~~ are influenced

by their parents.

both creative women and Pationate worker

7. My mother is ~~a woman who must use her creativity and she needs to work~~

~~with passion.~~

not only   and   but

8. When my father can't paint, he becomes angry, introverted, ~~and~~ he feels a lot

of frustration.

9. I wish I were more like my father, but I am not mechanical neither artistic.

10. I know that studying is more important than if I watch movies.

ⓐ Word Order

■ Embedded Questions

It is possible to combine a question with a statement or to combine two questions.
An **embedded question** is a question that is set within a larger sentence.

Question: What did the building cost?
Embedded question: The tourists wondered **what the building cost**.

In questions, if there is an auxiliary verb such as *do, did,* or *does,* it generally appears
before the subject. However, when a question is embedded in a larger sentence, remove
the auxiliary verb or place it after the subject. As you read the following examples,
pay attention to the word order in the embedded questions.

Combining Two Questions

Separate: Why **do** humans build skyscrapers? **Do** you know?
(In both questions, the helping verb is *do*.)

Combined: **Do** you know why humans build skyscrapers?
(The helping verb *do* is removed from the embedded question.)

Combining a Question and a Statement

Separate: What **should** <u>people</u> do during a fire? I wonder about it.
(In the question, the helping verb *should* appears before the subject.)

Combined: I wonder what <u>people</u> **should** do during a fire.
(In the embedded question, *should* is placed after the subject.)

Use the Correct Word Order

When you edit your writing, ensure that you have formed your embedded questions properly.

were
Otis wondered why ~~were~~ elevators ^ unreliable.

he did
I learned what ~~did he do.~~

EXERCISE 4

Make a new sentence from each question.

EXAMPLE: Why is the elevator stuck?   I wonder *why the elevator is stuck.*

1. Why is the alarm ringing?

Do you know _____

2. When will someone help us?

I wonder _____

3. What can we do?

Do you know *what* _____

4. Where is the phone?

Can you tell me *where the phone is?* _____

5. What did he say?

Can you hear _____

EXERCISE 5

Underline and correct nine errors in embedded questions.

elevators are
EXAMPLE: The writer explains why are elevators safe.

1. Before 1853, elevators were not reliable. Do you know why would people refuse

to enter an elevator? The hemp rope could break and the elevator could fall. You can

imagine why were people scared of elevators. Then in 1853, Elisha Otis had an

insight. Do you know what was his idea? Otis created a safety device out of two

hooks and a spring. When an elevator's rope became slack, the hooks would snap

into a guide rail and stop the elevator from falling.

2. Otis decided to enter the elevator business, but at first, he wasn't successful. He wondered why did nobody buy his elevators. Then, at the 1853 World's Fair in New York, he had the chance to show off his invention. Every day, Otis rose to the top of a shaft on his elevator. Then he instructed his helper to cut the cable with an axe. You can imagine why did the spectators scream. Instead of falling, the elevator jolted to a stop. Citizens wondered how did Otis survive. Soon, orders for Otis's safety elevator poured in.

3. Today, elevators are quite safe. In *The New Yorker*, Nick Paumgarten lists some elevator facts. First, do you know why does the close button rarely work? In fact, most elevators built since the 1990s have fake door-close buttons. Their purpose is to give people the illusion that they can control the elevator. Also, if an elevator falls, most people do not know what should they do. According to Otis's head of high-rise operations, Rick Pulling, jumping just before impact is not useful. You cannot jump fast enough to counteract the speed of the descent. Instead, do you know what can you do? Lie flat on the floor to distribute your weight.

■ *Present, Explain, and Describe*

Generally you should use *to* after the verbs *present*, *explain*, and *describe* when the action is being done to someone else. The preferred word order is the following:

> **present/explain/describe** *something* **to** <u>someone</u>

> *my colleague* **to** <u>you</u>
> I would like to **present** ~~you my colleague~~.

> *the process* **to** <u>you</u>
> Can I **describe** ~~you the process~~?

© PEARSON LONGMAN • REPRODUCTION PROHIBITED

EXERCISE 6

Underline and correct the word-order error in each sentence. Write "C" next to correct sentences.

EXAMPLE: I will explain <u>you my plans</u>.   *my plans to you*

1. Can you describe me a typical workday?   _____

2. I would like to present you my husband. _____

3. We will present you the survey results. _____

4. I want my doctor to explain me the problem. _____

5. When will you describe me my role? _____

6. Someone will explain the problem to you. _____

7. I should know why did he leave. _____

8. He will explain you his answer. _____

■ Frequency Adverbs

Frequency adverbs are words such as *sometimes*, *never*, *always*, *often*, *usually*, *daily*, *generally*, or *ever*. They indicate how often an action occurs. Place mid-sentence frequency adverbs in the following positions.

- After the verb *be*:

    The senator <u>is</u> **often** late.

- After auxiliary verbs*:

    He <u>has</u> **never** complained about his salary.

- Before all other present- and past-tense verbs:

    We **usually** <u>meet</u> on Saturdays.

EXERCISE **7**

Underline and correct nine word-order errors.

I will explain you an average workday. I arrive usually at eight-thirty in the morning and review the schedule. I see generally the first patient at about nine o'clock. I try usually to spend about ten minutes with each patient. However, I have spent often twenty minutes or more with patients who are especially worried. Although the clinic remains open until 5:00 p.m., walk-in clients never are permitted after 3:30 p.m. I must admit that I am forced frequently to remain until six or even seven o'clock in the evening. I have described you a very ordinary day. Most doctors do not complain, and they usually are very happy with their schedules.

---

* Auxiliary verbs are helping verbs that appear before the main verb (<u>has</u> seen, <u>would</u> have known, <u>is</u> going, etc.). They help to show a verb's tense, mood, or voice.

Answer the following questions. If necessary, go back and review the appropriate section.

1. Underline and correct the parallel structure error in each sentence.

   a) Accounting is not boring neither difficult.

   b) For my hobbies, I love cycling, swimming, and to hike.

   c) I would rather go swimming than reading.

2. Correct the embedded question error in each sentence.

   a) We have discussed what are the problems.

   b) I wonder how will you adapt to the new job.

   c) Do you know how busy can it be at income tax time?

3. Correct the word-order errors.

   a) When we met, the accountant described me various options.

   b) He explained me the tax penalties.

FINAL REVIEW

PART **A**

Underline and correct fifteen errors with parallel structure and word order.

> took out
> EXAMPLE: In my job, I served people, cleaned the kitchen, and I had to take out
> the trash.

1. I am applying for a job as an assistant store manager. I believe I am an ideal candidate

because I am creative, hard working, and I have energy. My three years of learning

about customers' needs have prepared me for this challenge. Perhaps you are

wondering what are my qualifications. In the next paragraphs, I will describe

you my background.

2. At my college, students learn usually about management, accounting, and finance. My previous co-workers, my fellow students, and the people who teach me can attest to my strong character. In my program, I learned to work hard and also communicating. Furthermore, in my part-time job as a waitress, I learned useful skills. I was always patient with my boss, the other employees, and when there were customers. Also, I learn things quickly. People do not have to explain me the rules more than once.

3. Truthfully, I would rather work with the public than working alone. In fact, I love interacting with customers because I am sociable, because I can practise my English, and I really like to help others. I believe the job as assistant store manager would be both interesting and a challenge. Please consider this application because I am not lazy neither rude. Also, I work quickly and efficient.

4. When we meet, I will describe you my other skills. You will realize how can I be an asset to your company.

PART B

Circle the letter of the correct answer.

5. Can you tell me ...

   a) what time it is?   **b)** what time is it?   **c)** what is the time?

6. Do you know what ... in the future?

   a) will you do   **b)** you will do   **c)** you do

7. Students should really consider what ...

   a) are the available jobs.   **b)** are the jobs available.   **c)** jobs are available.

8. I sometimes wonder who ...

   a) can I trust.   **b)** I can trust.   **c)** do I trust.

9. In our survey, we asked respondents ...

   a) when do they lie.   **b)** when did they lie.   **c)** when they lie.

a Verb Tenses

■ Present Tenses

The **simple present tense** indicates that an action is a general truth, a fact, or habitual activity. The present tense can also indicate a scheduled future action.

Fact: Jerome **sells** handmade furniture.
Habitual activity: The designers **buy** fabric every week.
Future action: The shipment **arrives** at 10:00 p.m.

The **present progressive tense** indicates that an action is in progress at this moment or for a temporary period of time. The present progressive can also indicate that an action will happen in the near future.

Now: The young politician **is speaking** about the economy.
Temporary activity: The new electric car **is selling** quickly these days.
Future action: We **are leaving** in ten minutes.

■ Past Tenses

The **simple past tense** indicates that an action began and ended before the present time. Use the same form for both singular and plural past tense verbs except for *be*, which has two past forms: *was* and *were*. If you cannot remember some irregular verb forms, consult Appendix 1.

Regular: Last March, the entrepreneurs **launched** their website.
Irregular: The company **sold** the patent a year ago.

The **past progressive tense** indicates that an action was in progress at a specific past time or was interrupted while in progress.

Activity in progress: At 2:00 p.m. yesterday, John **was presenting** his plans.
Interrupted activity: While they **were talking**, the power went out.

■ Future Tenses

The future tenses indicate that an action has not taken place yet. Generally, use *will* or *be going to* to indicate the future tense. In formal circumstances and in British English, the word *shall* can also be used to indicate the future, as in *I shall contact you*. In legal or formal documents, *shall* usually means that an action is mandatory: *The applicant shall possess a minimum of two years experience.* Keep in mind that the simple present and the present progressive can also indicate the future.

> Tomorrow, the directors **will have** a meeting.
> Future projects **are going to be** on the agenda.
> All employees **shall attend**.

The **future progressive** tense indicates that an action will be in progress at a specific future time. To form the future progressive tense, use *will be* + the *-ing* verb form.

> Do not call me tomorrow afternoon because I **will be presenting** my ideas.

TIP

Time Clauses

Never use the future tense in time clauses; use the present tense instead. Time clauses are introduced by the following time markers:

| after | as long as | as soon as | before | by the time |
| in case | unless | until | when | while |

time clause
I will call you <u>when **I finish** work</u>.

■ Present Perfect Tenses

The **present perfect tense** is formed with *have* or *has* and the past participle. It is used in two distinct ways.

1. Use the present perfect to show that an action began in the past and continues to the present time. You will often use *since* and *for* with this tense.

   > Kate **has been** a marketing manager <u>for</u> nine years.
   > <u>Since</u> 2001, the products **have sold** extremely well.

2. Use the present perfect to show that one or more completed actions occurred at unknown or unspecified past times.

   > Kate **has been** to Bosnia.
   > Ms. Robitaille **has visited** China twice.

The **present perfect progressive** is formed with *have been* or *has been* + the *-ing* verb form. It indicates that an action has been in progress from a past time up until the present moment. This tense emphasizes the duration of the uninterrupted activity or shows that the results of an action are still visible.

> Kevin **has been speaking** for twenty minutes. When will he stop speaking?
> Somebody **has been using** my computer. It is still warm.

TIP

Using the *-ing* Form

With some verbs, such as *live, work, teach,* and *study,* the present perfect and the present perfect progressive tenses have essentially the same meaning.

> Ian **has been working** here for a week.
> Ian **has worked** here for a week.

■ Choosing the Simple Past or the Present Perfect

Look at the difference between the past and the present perfect tenses.

Simple past: In 2002, Ms. Robitaille **went** to Shanghai.
                   (This event occurred at a known past time.)

Present perfect: Since 2002, she **has owned** a factory in China.
                   (The action began in the past and continues to the present.)
                   She **has made** many business contacts.
                   (Making business contacts occurred at unknown past times.)

TIP

Present Perfect Usage

- Use the past tense when referring to someone who is no longer living. Only use the present perfect tense when the action has a relationship to someone or something that still exists.

                   wrote
      Kurt Cobain ~~has written~~ many great songs.

- Use key words to help you decide what tense to use. Be careful: when the past time is stated and other sentences give details about that past time, use the past tense.

      Selvan **has been** a reporter <u>since</u> he graduated from college. Four years <u>ago</u>, he **moved** to Toronto. He **wrote** for *The Globe and Mail*, and he **published** a collection of stories.

■ Past Perfect Tenses

The **past perfect tense** is formed with *had* and the past participle. It indicates that an action occurred before another past action.

      The meeting **had started** when Omar arrived.

The **past perfect progressive** indicates that an action was in progress, without interruption, before another past action occurred. To form the past perfect progressive, use *had been* + verb + *-ing*.

      When I returned home, I realized that somebody **had been using** my computer. It was still warm.

■ Future Perfect Tenses

The **future perfect tense** is formed with *will have* or *(be) going to have* and the past participle. It indicates that an action will occur before or up to the time of another future action.

      By the year end, we **will have hired** over fifty new employees.

The **future perfect progressive** indicates that an action will be in progress, without interruption, up to a future time. Form this tense with *will have* + verb + *-ing*.

      By Sunday, I **will have been working** for thirty hours on this project.

Verb Tense Timeline

Verb tense indicates when an action occurred. The following timeline shows the main verb tenses.

PAST TIME	TODAY	FUTURE TIME

Past Perfect
(A past action occurred before another past time.)
We left because we **had** already **seen** the show.

Present Perfect
(A past action was repeated and the times are unknown.)
Alex **has met** the client twice.
(A past action continues to the present.)
We **have worked** here since 2003.

Future Perfect
(A future action occurs up to or before another future action.)
By next May, Ann **will have worked** here for twenty years.

Past Progressive
(A past action was in progress and was interrupted.)
I **was typing** when the phone rang.

Present Progressive
(An action is happening now.)
I **am relaxing** right now.

Future Progressive
(An action will be happening at a future time.)
Kate **will be working** when you call her tonight.

Simple Past
(An action finished at a definite past time.)
Yesterday the office **opened** at 9:00 a.m.

Simple Present
(An action is a general fact or habit.)
Jay always **sells** the most products.

Future Tenses
(An action will occur at a future date.)
We **will leave** soon.
We **are going to leave** soon.

Write the correct tense of the verb *be* in the blank.

EXAMPLE: Dana Fong _____is_____ a human rights lawyer.

1. These days, Ms. Fong _____ a junior partner in her law firm. Ms. Fong

_____ a lawyer since 2003.

2. Last year, she _____ busy with a high-profile criminal case. Her clients

_____ two men accused of embezzling funds. One of them

_____ in trouble with the law several times before the case went to trial.

3. Two months from now, she _____ in Jamaica for her vacation. She will

contact you when she _____ ready to discuss your case.

4. By next December 31, she _____ in Montreal for ten years.

Complete the sentences with the correct form of the verbs in parentheses.

EXAMPLE: Mr. Slater (work) _____has worked_____ as a police officer since 1990.

1. (you, ever, want) _____ to be your own boss?

There (be) _____ over 2 million small businesses in Canada.

2. In 1996, Jim Slater (be) _____

a police officer with the Winnipeg Police

Service. As a canine handler, Slater

(take) _____ care of police

dogs. One day, while he (head)

_____ into a high-risk

confrontation, he noticed that the officers were protected by body armour, but

the police dogs were not. Slater wanted to find a vest that could protect his dog Olaf,

but all the vests on the market (be) _____ too bulky.

3. In 1997, Slater decided to invent something that he (never, see)

_____ before: lightweight body armour for dogs. At that

time, he (know, not) _____ how to sew, but with his

wife's help, he (make) _____ a vest for his dog using

his own old body armour. By the end of 1997, several other officers (ask)

_____ Slater to provide custom-made vests for their dogs.

4. The Slaters, who (think, never) _____ about owning a business before then, decided to patent their dog vest. Since 1998, their company, named K9 Storm, (grow) _____ tremendously. Today, K9 Storm (produce) _____ the vests in a Winnipeg manufacturing plant.

5. By next January, the company (sell) _____ dog vests to more than twelve nations. Glori Slater says, "We (save) _____ the lives of many police dogs." Next week, when Glori Slater (visit) _____ Italy, she will present K9 Storm's latest line of protective dog vests.

EXERCISE 3

Underline the correct form of the verbs in parentheses.

> EXAMPLE: In the 1960s, some American companies (<u>attempted</u> / have attempted) to enter the Japanese marketplace.

1. (Did you ever hear / Have you ever heard) of General Mills? The company (existed / has existed / is existing) since 1856 and (produce / produces) many food brands, including Green Giant, Pillsbury, and Betty Crocker.

2. Each year, General Mills (is selling / sell / sells) products around the world. Joyce Millet is an author who (writes / is writing / has been writing) for over twenty years. In 2004, Millet (published / has published / has been publishing) an article called "Marketing in Japan: What History Can Teach Us." Her article (has described / describes) examples of product failures.

3. In 1968, General Mills (was deciding / decided) to market Betty Crocker cake mixes in Japan. The year before, most Japanese consumers (have never heard / had never heard) of Betty Crocker because nobody (has ever marketed / had ever marketed) the mixes in Asia.

4. In 1968, very few Japanese homes (have / had / were having) ovens. Designers at General Mills (was / were / have been) unsure how people would bake the cakes. At that time, most Japanese homes (contain / contained / had contained) a rice cooker, so designers created a spongy cake mix that could bake in a rice cooker.

5. In November 1968, sales of the Betty Crocker cake mix (was / were / have been) good, but sales quickly tumbled. The problem was simple. At that time, most Japanese citizens (believed / have believed) that rice was sacred, and they (didn't want / haven't wanted) the cake flavour to contaminate the rice. Since then, General Mills (withdrew / has withdrawn / had withdrawn) Betty Crocker cake mixes from Japan.

Underline and correct ten verb errors.

EXAMPLE: The Coca-Cola Company has ~~begun~~ *began* in 1886.

1. Since 1886, Coca-Cola is a familiar product throughout the world. By the year 2000, the company made some very successful marketing decisions. In 1931, Haddon Sundblom has illustrated a Coca-Cola advertisement with a Santa Claus figure that had a white beard, rosy cheeks, and a red suit. Since then, Sundblom's drawing is the popular image of the Christmas character.

2. Although the Coca-Cola Company been very successful since its inception, occasionally it has made blunders. In 1984, Coca-Cola managers have worried about the increasing popularity of Pepsi. That year, Coke developers modified the original formula and maked the product much sweeter.

3. On April 23, 1985, at a press conference, Coca-Cola's chairman has introduced New Coke by calling it "smoother, rounder, and bolder." Unfortunately, when the product hit store shelves, consumers complained about the taste. So, on July 29, 1985, the company pulled New Coke from the shelves and reintroduced the original product, calling it Coke Classic. Curiously, Coke Classic is very successful since its reintroduction. Since the New Coke fiasco, other companies have learn from Coca-Cola's mistake. If consumers love a product, do not modify it!

Tense Consistency

A verb tense gives your readers an idea about the time that an event occurred. A **tense shift** occurs when you shift from one tense to another for no logical reason. When you write, ensure that your tenses are consistent and that any shifts are logical.

Tense shift: The company **refused** to accept the shipment of fruit because the bananas **are** overripe.

Correct: The company **refused** to accept the shipment of fruit because the bananas **were** overripe.
          (At the time of the shipping, they were overripe.)

TIP

Would and *Could*

When you tell a story about a past event, use *would* instead of *will* and *could* instead of *can*.

couldn't

In 2001, Simon Brault wanted to be an actor. At that time, he ~~can't~~ find a good acting

would

job. To earn extra cash, he ~~will~~ deliver telegrams wearing a costume.

EXERCISE 5

Underline and correct the *would* and *could* errors, verb errors, or tense shifts. There are twelve errors.

like

EXAMPLE: Consumer groups didn't <u>liked</u> the marketing campaign.

1. In previous centuries, some mothers can't breastfeed, so they fed their children cow's milk. In 1838, a German physician decided that he will analyze cow's milk on a regular basis. He was discovering that cow's milk had large proteins and low levels of carbohydrates, so it was not a healthy alternative to breast milk. Later, in the 1870s, there has been a scientific breakthrough, and the Nestlé company produced the first infant formula. Consumers just had to mixed water with the formula.

2. A century later, in 1973, Nestlé decided to sell the formula in Africa. The company was putting advertisements on billboards. At that time, Nestlé will give free samples to African women as soon as they had their babies. In hospitals, mothers seen their own breast milk dry up after they gave formula to their babies. When the women returned home, they did not had enough money to continue buying enough formula.

They added too much water to the formula, and the water is often contaminated. Babies who drunk formula become malnourished. In many villages, the level of infant malnutrition and mortality rised.

Question Forms

In questions, word order is usually reversed. If a sentence has an auxiliary verb, place it before the subject.

<u>They</u> **should** sign the contract. ➡ **Should** <u>they</u> sign the contract?
<u>The client</u> **will** arrive at noon. ➡ **Will** <u>the client</u> arrive at noon?
<u>We</u> **have** already met. ➡ **Have** <u>we</u> already met?

In the simple present tense, start a question with *do* or *does*. In the simple past, use *did*. If the main verb is *be*, simply place *be* before the subject.

Present tense: <u>Consumers</u> love the product. ➡ **Do** <u>they</u> love the product?
<u>The new brand</u> costs a lot. ➡ **Does** <u>it</u> cost a lot?
<u>The café</u> **is** closed. ➡ **Is** <u>the café</u> closed?
Past tense: <u>She</u> sold her business. ➡ **Did** <u>she</u> sell her business?
<u>The owner</u> **was** too busy. ➡ **Was** <u>the owner</u> too busy?

TIP

Use the Base Form after *Do* and *To*

Remember to use the base form of verbs that follow
* *do* (*does*, *did*) in question and negative forms;
* the word *to* (infinitive form).

$\quad\quad\quad\quad\quad\quad\quad\quad$ hire $\quad\quad\quad\quad\quad\quad\quad\quad\quad\quad\quad\quad$ interview
Mr. Kamry wanted **to** ~~hired~~ a new manager. **Did** he ~~interviewed~~ many candidates?

EXERCISE **6**

Fill in the blanks with the correct auxiliary from the following list. Some of the words can be used more than once, and some words will not appear in the answers.

do	does	did	is	am	are	was	were	have	has	will

EXAMPLE: _____*Do*_____ some brands sell better than others?

1. How much influence _____ brand names have on consumers?

2. _____ you ever bought a product because of the brand name?

3. Last year, why _____ many companies on the brink of bankruptcy?

4. _____ Dove market its soaps to older women?

5. Since 2000, which soap product _____ been the most successful?

6. Last month, _____ you buy soap?

7. Right now, which brand of soap _____ next to your bathtub?

8. _____ the average driver notice the billboards on highways?

9. When you were a child, which products _____ you want to have?

10. In the future, _____ advertising affect your buying choices?

EXERCISE **7**

Students were asked to prepare questions for an interview with a professional. They made errors in verb tense and word order. They also made errors in the question words. Correct the underlined errors.

How often

EXAMPLE: <u>How many times</u> do you go on business trips?

1. <u>Since when are you</u> a broker?

2. Does this job <u>included</u> a lot of teamwork?

3. At <u>witch</u> university did you study?

4. <u>How</u> does the schedule of a broker <u>looks</u> like?

5. <u>Is</u> there opportunities to advance in your company?

6. How <u>much</u> hours <u>are you working</u> in a typical week?

7. <u>Does a therapist can</u> work at home?

8. <u>Is</u> there security risks in your job?

9. <u>How long time do you work</u> at your job?

10. <u>Does your schedule is</u> flexible?

11. How long <u>you have been</u> with the company?

12. <u>For how many times</u> are you expected to work on weekends?

Answer the following questions. If necessary, go back and review the appropriate section.

1. What is the difference between *has seen* and *had seen*?

_____

_____

2. Underline and correct the verb errors in the following sentences. There may be one or two errors in each sentence.

a) Since 2001, millions of people bought clothing online.

b) Five years ago, Pat Chen was owning a clothing store.

c) Since 2005, the company has hire a lot of people.

d) By the time Anna sold her shares in the company, she made a lot of money.

e) When I will have some extra cash, I will investing in an online company.

FINAL REVIEW

PART A

Write the correct form of the verb in parentheses.

EXAMPLE: Since 1980, many women (decide) _____*have decided*_____ to work in construction.

1. In the summer of 2000, Janet Rickstrew and Mary Tatum (be) _____

in the middle of a renovation project. One of the women mentioned that she

(see, never) _____ a nice-looking tool belt. Then they

complained about the lack of tools made for women's hands. That day, they

(have) _____ the great idea of creating tools for females.

Since 2000, they (sell) _____ products such as pink

hammers and power drills. By 2007, their company, Tomboy Tools, (expand)

_____ into three countries.

2. In March 2007, Marissa McTasney wanted to start her own construction company,

so she (take) _____ a course called "Women in Skilled Trades."

The teacher (give) _____ the students vouchers for work boots.

Marissa wanted pink boots, but none existed. Since then, she (develop)

_____ pink work boots, hard hats, and safety glasses.

Her company, Moxie Trades, (be) _____ very successful since

its inception. Next year, when McTasney (have) _____ some new

products, she will market them at trade shows.

PART B

Underline and correct five errors with tenses.

3. According to the *Toronto Star*, women does about half of all home renovations.

In fact, as recently as 1999, hardware stores didn't considered the needs of women.

Yet since the 1980s, women been spending a lot of money at hardware stores.

In the past, established companies were not making women's tools. Today, many

hardware stores are having special products for females.

PART C

Underline and correct any errors in question forms. Write "C" next to correct
sentences.

4. Why do advertising is so successful?

5. What products do the average citizen need?

6. Since 2000, which marketing campaign has been the most successful?

7. What new products did Marissa designed in 2007?

8. Since last summer, how many tools you have bought?

UNIT 9
MODALS AND MOOD

 ## Modal Auxiliaries

Modals are helping verbs that express possibility, advice, and so on. Review the present and past forms of the following modals.

Function	Modal	Past Form	Example
Ability	**can** run	**could** run	He **could** run extremely fast when he was young.
Necessity	**must** study **have to** work	**had to** study **had to** work	Kirk **had to** study last night. He **had to** work yesterday.
Probability	**must** be	**must have** been	Yesterday, Kate **must have** been at home.
Advice	**should** leave **ought to** leave	**should have** left **ought to have** left	He **should have** left earlier. He **ought to have** left earlier.
Possibility	**could** stay **might** do **may** help	**could have** stayed **might have** done **may have** helped	Dan **could have** stayed with you. Britney **might have** done it. Jay **may have** helped her.
Conditional Desire	**would** tell **would** like	**would have** told **would have** liked	If I had known, I **would have** told you. I **would have** liked to meet Mozart.

■ *Must* and *Have To*

In affirmative sentences, *must* and *have to* mean essentially the same thing. However, in negative sentences, they have distinct meanings.

Positive: We **must** leave. = We **have to** leave.

Negative: You **must not** leave. = It is forbidden.
You **don't have to** leave. = There is no obligation to leave.

Also, remember that *must* can indicate an obligation or a probability.

• When *must* means "it is necessary," the past form is *had to*.

She **must** work late.   She **had to** work late.

• When *must* means "it is probable," the past form is *must have* + the past participle.

He **must** <u>be</u> tired.   He **must have** <u>been</u> tired.

Write the past form of the bold verb phrases.

PRESENT   **PAST**

EXAMPLE: Eric **should apply** for the job.   *should have applied*

1. Jade **can't understand** sign language.   _____

2. Perhaps she **could find** a job working
with the hearing impaired.   _____

3. She **has to learn** sign language.   _____

4. Maybe she **should practise** more
often.   _____

5. She **must find** a job.   _____

6. She **may borrow** some money.   _____

7. Jade had an accident. She **should see**
a doctor.   _____

8. Look at her leg! It **must hurt**.   _____

■ Avoiding Modal Errors

Never add *-ing*, *-ed*, or *-s* to verbs that follow modals.

    study
We should ~~studied~~ the problem.

Use standard past forms. Some people say *should of* or *shoulda*. These are non-standard forms and you should avoid using them, especially in written communication. When you use the past forms of *should*, *would*, and *could*, always include *have* + the past participle.

    should have learned
When he did business in Japan, he ~~shoulda learn~~ about Japanese business etiquette.

Underline and correct five modal errors.

    should learn
EXAMPLE: You should <u>learning</u> about business cards.

When you make a business card, you should studied various options. According to

experts, a business card can presents a positive or negative image. First, you should make

sure your card is up to date. Two years ago, Chantal Cyr printed two thousand business

cards. When she moved, she should of made new cards but she didn't bother. Now, when she hands out cards, she updates them by writing over the old phone number. Honestly, nobody would thinking she is very professional. Last week, she coulda made a better impression on a client if she had given him an updated business card.

Mood

In sentences expressing a strong demand, a wish, or a condition, the verb requires special treatment. Carefully review the following rules.

■ Expressing a Necessity or Demand

Some expressions of necessity require a dependent clause beginning with *that*. In such sentences, use the base form of the verb in the dependent clause. Notice that you use *be* instead of *is*, *am*, or *are* in the dependent clause.

Present: It is absolutely necessary <u>that she **arrive** on time</u>.
(not *arrives*)

I insist <u>that everyone **be** present at the meeting</u>.
(not *is*)

Past: I demanded <u>that Eric **receive** a second chance</u>.
(not *received*)

Future: I will insist <u>that we **be** treated with respect</u>.
(not *are* or *will be*)

■ Expressing a Wish

You make a wish when you want to change your reality. Review how to form sentences expressing a wish.

- **Wish about the Present**

  When you wish about a present situation, use the past tense.

  I wish I **had** better marks in chemistry.

  When you wish to change a habit, use *would* or *could*.

  I wish you **would** stop biting your nails.

  With the verb *be*, always use *were* in formal English. (In spoken English, you may hear *was*.)

  He wishes that he **were** younger.

- **Wish about the Past**

  When you wish you could change a past situation, use the past perfect tense.

  I wish that I **had passed** my high school math course.

TIP

Hope or *Wish*

When you want to change a fact, use *wish*. When you express a desire, use *hope*. Don't use *wish* with the present tense.

I **hope** I finish this project soon. I **wish** the project were not so long!

Underline the correct word in parentheses.

> **EXAMPLE:** I wish it (is / was / <u>were</u>) summer.

1. Last year, I paid for my new car with a credit card. Now I regret it. I really (hope / wish) that I (did not spend / had not spent) so much money. Every month, I have to make large payments. My wife also has a credit card, and she loves buying things with it. Yesterday, she put another $1000 on the card. I wish that she (is / are / was / were) more careful with her spending. Unfortunately, we are not frugal.

2. This morning, I phoned the credit card company. I insisted that the company (reduce / reduces) the interest rate. The woman on the phone laughed at me. Then I became really angry and I demanded that she (transfer / transfers) me to her superior. I am upset because the credit card company (charge / charges) 19 percent interest when the lending rate is only two percent.

3. We should demand that the government (take / takes) action. I wish that our prime minister (are / was / were) easier to contact. It is impossible to speak directly with such leaders. I (wish / hope) that our next leader is better than the current one.

■ Expressing a Condition (Using *If*)

• Possible Present or Future

Use the "possible" form when the condition is true or possible.

If + present tense	present or future tense
If you **think** about it,	life **is** wonderful.
If you **worry** too much,	you **will make** yourself sick.

• Unlikely Present

Use the "unlikely" form when the condition is improbable and probably won't happen.

If + past tense	*would* (expresses a condition)
	could (expresses a possibility)
If you **knew** Miguel,	you **would love** him.
If I **won** a million dollars,	I **could quit** my job.

• Impossible Past

When a condition is impossible because the time has passed, use the past perfect tense in the *if* clause.

If + past perfect tense	*would have* (+ past participle)
	could have (+ past participle)
If you **had invited** me,	I **would have** <u>come</u> to the meeting.
If my father **had lived** a little longer, he **could have** <u>met</u> his grandson.	

Write the correct form of the verb in parentheses.

> **EXAMPLE:** If I (know) _____*had known*_____ about the price change, I would have cancelled my reservation.

1. If you (visit) _____ the Bryant Hotel, you will probably meet

Thomas Hine. Hine is a desk clerk at the hotel. It is a beautiful place, and the rooms have a view of the sea. Honestly, if I (have)

_____ some time off right now,

I would go there. However, I cannot take

a holiday right now. Perhaps if I (be)

_____ able to quit my job, I could

take a vacation, but I can't quit. I need the work.

2. Yesterday, when a customer asked to change rooms, Thomas was very rude to her.

The customer complained to the manager. If Thomas (be) _____

pleasant, perhaps the customer (not, complain) _____

_____. However, because Thomas acted in an unprofessional manner,

his job is now on the line. Thomas had a migraine yesterday. Perhaps he (avoid)

_____ the problem if he (stay) _____

home yesterday instead of going to work. This afternoon, Thomas has

to speak with his manager. If Thomas explains the circumstances, perhaps the

manager (permit) _____ him to keep his job.

Underline and correct twelve errors with modals and mood.

                   had done

EXAMPLE: If he <u>would have done</u> some research, he would have found the answer.

1. If you will search on the Internet, you will find information about patents and

trademarks. In 2004, Raul Lopez and I created an exercise machine. Raul insisted

that we applied for a patent. We believed that nobody could copy our invention if

we patent it. So we paid a lot of money for a patent, and we named the machine

Body Challenge. A few months later, someone else made a similar machine

and named it Body Challenge.

2. Unfortunately, we did not have a trademark. If we would have paid for a trademark,

our idea would have been protected. Nobody could have use the same product name.

Perhaps if we woulda spoken with a lawyer, we would of saved a lot of time and

money. I really wish we met with a lawyer sooner! If we would have owned

the Body Challenge name, nobody else could have took the same name. Tamara

Monosoff, an inventor, says that trademarks are less expensive and more useful than patents. If she had to choose between a trademark and a patent, she pay for a trademark. I guess, back in 2004, we shoulda done more research before we launched our product!

Underline and correct the errors in the following sentences. Then write a rule to explain the error. If necessary, go back and review the appropriate section.

1. I wish your new job will make you happy.

Rule: _____

2. We shoulda met with an accountant last week.

Rule: _____

3. If you would have asked for help, I would have given it to you.

Rule: _____

4. The judge demanded that the company rehired the employee.

Rule: _____

5. I did not pay my income taxes last year. Now I have to pay a penalty. I wish I paid my taxes last year!

Rule: _____

FINAL REVIEW

PART A

Underline the correct answer in parentheses.

EXAMPLE: Monique (<u>hopes</u> / wishes) that her father will buy her new clothing.

1. Thirteen-year-old Monique insists that her father (buy / buys) brand name clothing. Her father Kevin (wish / wishes / hopes) that his daughter (be / are / were) more reasonable. Last Friday, Monique demanded that her father (pay / paid) for expensive jeans. He should (refused / have refused / had refused). Honestly, if she (ask / would have asked / had asked) me for money, I would not have (give / gave / given) it to her. If I (would have been / were / had been) at the store that Friday, I (would tell / would had told / would have told) Monique to choose less expensive jeans. Kevin really (hopes / wishes) that his daughter will be more sensible in the future.

2. If Monique (was / were / would be) my child, I (was / were / would be) very strict. I would insist that she (acted / acts / act) in a more mature manner. In the future, if I (will have / have) children, I (try / will try / tried) not to spoil them.

PART B

Underline and correct five errors with modals or conditionals.

EXAMPLE: I wish that I <u>know</u> the answer.
knew

3. Alex Reed wants to find a job but he has made some mistakes. First, he sent out his résumé last week, but it was full of spelling errors. If he would have taken a bit of time to proofread it, he would have been able to fix many of the errors. Then, he went to a job interview yesterday and arrived late. People should always arriving on time for job interviews. Furthermore, Alex wore a stained T-shirt. He really shoulda worn a clean button-down shirt. Mrs. Cantin, the recruiter, mentioned the errors in Alex's résumé, and he was so embarrassed. He really wished that he asked someone to check it. Alex has another interview next week. I really wish he wears a clean shirt and pants for that interview!

UNIT 10
VERB AGREEMENT AND VOICE

 Subject-Verb Agreement

■ General Rules

Review the following subject-verb agreement rules.

- Present-tense verbs that follow third-person singular forms (*he, she, it*) take the *-s* or *-es* ending.

    My aunt <u>lives</u> alone and <u>has</u> a cat.

- Compound subjects joined by *and* take the plural form of the verb.

    The desk *and* **the computer** <u>are</u> in the stock room.

    However, if the compound subjects refer to a singular idea (the same person or thing), use a singular verb.

    The secretary and treasurer <u>is</u> Elaine Bennet.
    The horse and buggy <u>was</u> a common means of transportation.

    The phrases *as well as* and *along with* are not the same as *and*. The subject is before the interrupting expression.

    Ms. Baker, *as well as* the other clients, <u>demands</u> action.

- When subjects are joined by *or* or *nor*, the verb agrees with the subject closest to it.

    Neither the manager *nor* **the supervisor** <u>likes</u> the proposal.
    Either the doctor *or* **the nurses** <u>speak</u> with the patients.

■ Special Subject Forms

- Sometimes a gerund (the *-ing* form of a verb) is the singular subject of a sentence.
  Marketing <u>is</u> an interesting field.

- Indefinite pronouns beginning with *every-*, *some-*, *any-*, and *no-* are considered singular. Examples are *somebody, nothing, anyone, something*, and *everywhere*.

    Everybody <u>needs</u> friends.
    Nothing <u>surprises</u> me.

- Collective nouns refer to a group and are generally singular. Some examples of collective nouns are *army, association, audience, club, company, family, government, population*, and *public*.

    The **government** <u>collects</u> taxes.

Exception: When the members of the collective noun act individually, use the plural form of the verb.

> The **committee** have taken their seats.
> (*Members* is implied)

- An amount of something (money, distance, time, degrees, and so on) is singular when it is expressed as one unit and plural when it refers to individual units.

> **Fifteen dollars** <u>is</u> a fair price for that shirt.
> **Four hours** <u>is</u> a long time to wait.
>
> **Fifteen dollars** <u>are</u> in the tip jar.
> **Four hours** <u>have</u> passed and I am hungry.

- When nouns ending in *-ics* (*statistics, economics, politics, athletics, mathematics, logistics*) refer to a whole unit or a course of study, they are singular. When they refer to individual pieces of information, they are plural.

> **Politics** <u>is</u> a dirty business.
> **Statistics** <u>is</u> a difficult course.
>
> His family **politics** <u>are</u> none of my business.
> The **statistics** <u>show</u> that the candidate may lose the election.

T I P

Sentences Beginning with *Here* and *There*

When a sentence begins with *Here* or *There*, the subject is after the verb.

> *There* <u>are</u> many **employees** in the staff room.

EXERCISE 1

Underline the appropriate verb in each sentence.

> **EXAMPLE:** Statistics (<u>suggest</u> / suggests) that the business will be successful.

1. Everybody (want / wants) to be successful, and Ben Cathers is no exception.

2. Cathers, along with his friend Kyle Wilson, (was / were) just twelve years old when he started his web marketing business.

3. His company, which (was / were) small, originally had just two employees.

4. Eight hundred dollars (is / are) not a lot of money to launch a business.

5. Mathematics (is / are) not Ben's favourite subject.

6. Today, Ben Cathers, along with his brother and two friends, (control / controls) a successful business.

7. Either Cathers or Wilson (update / updates) the web page weekly.

8. Nobody representing the tax department (have / has) called Cathers.

9. Every day, either Wilson or his assistants (answer / answers) the phone.

10. Selling items such as pants and shirts online (require / requires) a lot of work.

11. Ben's family (were / was) not surprised by his success.

12. Today, Cathers and Wilson Inc. (is / are) a successful business.

■ Prepositional Phrases

A prepositional phrase consists of a preposition and an object, such as *over the moon*, *with help*, and *on his own*. Generally, the object of a prepositional phrase is not the subject of the sentence. In the following sentences, the subject and verb are separated by a prepositional phrase.

	prepositional phrase	
The clothing **company**	with two subsidiaries	<u>has</u> closed.
One	of your most useful traits	<u>is</u> patience.
Each	of the employees	<u>has</u> an office.

T I P

Look for the Subject

When trying to make the subject and verb agree, identify the subject. Sometimes a long prepositional phrase can be confusing.

The **smoke** from the pipes at the power plant <u>is</u> bad for the environment.

■ Indefinite Pronouns

Indefinite pronouns refer to a general person, place, or thing. Carefully review the following list of indefinite pronouns.

Indefinite Pronouns					
Singular	another anybody anyone anything	each everybody everyone everything	nobody no one nothing one	other somebody someone something	either neither another much
Plural	both, few, many, others, several				

If an indefinite pronoun appears before the prepositional phrase, the subject agrees with the indefinite pronoun.

Singular subject: **Neither** of the students <u>is</u> available.
Plural subject: **Both** of the students <u>are</u> busy.

Exceptions

Some indefinite pronouns and expressions of quantity don't follow the preceding rule.

The following indefinite pronouns can be singular or plural, depending on the item that they refer to. Remember that non-count nouns such as *information*, *money*, *evidence*, and *homework* are always singular.

> all   any   none   more   most   some

Singular subject: **Some** of the money is missing.
  (*Some* refers to *money*, which is a singular non-count noun.)

Plural subject: **Some** of the accounts have closed.
  (*Some* refers to *accounts*, which is plural.)

Also be careful with fractions, percentages, and the words *majority* or *minority*. They can be singular or plural, depending on the object that they refer to.

Singular subject: **Two-thirds** of the information <u>has</u> been sent.
  (*Two-thirds* refers to *information*, which is a singular non-count noun.)

Plural subject: **Two-thirds** of our clients <u>have</u> been contacted.
  (*Two-thirds* refers to *clients*, which is plural.)

10

Circle the subject of each sentence. Then underline the correct verb form.

EXAMPLE: There (is / <u>are</u>) many (companies) that sell pesticides.

1. One of the most controversial issues in our society (is / are) lawn maintenance.
In past decades, homeowners (was / were) expected to have beautiful green lawns.
In most regions, there (was / were) thousands of lawn companies. Additionally,
products such as the herbicide Weed 'N Feed (was / were) popular. The use of
herbicides and pesticides (was / were) common.

2. Since 2003, the province of Quebec (have /
has) had a pesticide ban. Phase three of the
ban (was / were) passed in 2009. Although
both Killex and WeedEx (is / are) popular
in Ontario, neither of those products (is /
are) available in Quebec. Therefore, one of
North America's strongest anti-pesticide
laws (exist / exists) in Quebec. Every home
gardener, as well as each lawn care

company, (is / are) no longer able to use 210 different lawn care products. In fact,
of the most toxic products, about 95 percent (is / are) no longer available in stores.

3. In Montreal, the Cloutier family, along with Edward and Carol Webb, (hate / hates)
the ban. Both families (love / loves) to have green lawns. Sometimes, either Myriam
or her brother (has / have) to pull out the dandelions. In the spring, most of their
leisure time (is / are) spent doing that chore. Nonetheless, in Quebec, about
three-quarters of the population (support / supports) the ban. The minority of
citizens (break / breaks) the laws.

Underline and correct any errors in subject-verb agreement. Write "C" next to correct
sentences.

       wants
 EXAMPLE: Everybody <u>want</u> to succeed.

1. My sister has many business ideas, and every one of her ideas are original.

2. However, neither of us are good at accounting.

3. There is several mistakes young entrepreneurs make.

4. Sometimes, people doesn't know who their customers are.

5. About one-half of companies has a marketing budget that is too small.

6. Anybody who has great products need a promotions budget.

7. There is some business people who don't target their marketing effectively.

8. When an optician placed advertisements in a teen magazine, she was hoping to sell eyeglasses.

9. She forgot that the majority of the reading audience were too young to pay for eyeglasses.

10. Every entrepreneur needs to develop a marketing plan.

11. Statistics shows that many small businesses are not well planned.

12. The minority of small business owners makes a business plan.

 # Active and Passive Voice

In sentences that use the **active voice**, the subject performs the action. In the **passive voice**, the subject receives the action. To form the passive voice, use the appropriate tense of the verb *be* plus the past participle. Look carefully at the following two sentences.

Active: The student **posted** a video about solar energy on YouTube.
(This is active, because the subject, *student*, performed the action.)

Passive: A video about solar energy **was posted** on YouTube.
(This is passive because the subject, *video*, was affected by the action and did not perform the action.)

Verb Tenses	Voice	
	Active (The subject performs the action.)	**Passive** (The subject receives the action.) *be* + past participle
Simple present:	We write ads.	Ads **are written** (by them).
Present progressive:	We are writing ads.	Ads **are being written**.
Simple past:	We wrote ads.	Ads **were written**.
Present perfect:	We have written ads.	Ads **have been written**.
Future:	We will write ads.	Ads **will be written**.
Modals:	We can write ads.	Ads **can be written**.
	We could write ads.	Ads **could be written**.
	We should write ads.	Ads **should be written**.
	We could have written ads.	Ads **could have been written**.
	We should have written ads.	Ads **should have been written**.

Write the verb in the passive voice. Use the suggested verb and/or modal. Ensure that you use the correct tense.

EXAMPLE: A lot of articles (post) _____ *are posted* _____ on the Internet each day.

1. Every day, bias (show) _____ by many journalists.

A particular word (can / use) _____ to

manipulate readers. For example, in January 2009, citizens (influence) _____

_____ by the use of the word *anarchists* to describe

a group of environmentalists. The article (write) _____

by a former politician. He did not write with objectivity. The word *activists*

(could / use) _____ in the article instead.

2. People (should not / sway) _____ by

everything they read in newspapers or online. Sometimes a small incident (blow)

_____ out of proportion by bloggers and online news sites.

Many global warming deniers, for instance, (give) _____

a tremendous gift with 2009's "climate e-mail" scandal. A hacker posted e-mails from

climate scientists. In November, 2009, the e-mails (present) _____

_____ as proof of a conspiracy among scientists.

3. In December, 2009, restraint (could / show) _____

by journalists and bloggers, but many showed no moderation. Instead, headlines

(publish) _____ proclaiming that global

warming was false. Today, a lot of climate-warming evidence (view) _____

_____ with skepticism by members of the public.

■ Choosing the Active or Passive Voice

Generally, in business writing, try to use the active voice instead of the passive voice. The active voice is more direct and friendly than the passive voice. For example, read these two versions of a message.

Passive voice: Your complaint has been analyzed by us and steps will be taken to solve the problem. You will be contacted by our sales representative.

Active voice: We have analyzed your complaint and will take steps to solve the problem. Our sales representative will contact you.

Exception: When you write a report based on survey results, research, or scientific findings, it is best to not refer to yourself. By using the passive voice, the *data* rather than the actor takes precedence.

The *by* ... Phrase

In many passive sentences, it is not necessary to write the *by* ... phrase.

The survey was conducted in 2009 ~~by me~~.

EXERCISE 5

Underline five examples of the passive voice in the following letter. Then rewrite the letter using the active voice.

Dear Mr. Wilson,

Your letter has been received by me, and your offer will be reviewed. The terms will be analyzed by my lawyer. Then you will be contacted by my secretary. I hope that a suitable agreement can be reached by us.

_____

_____

_____

_____

EXERCISE 6

Write the passive form of each sentence. Respect the verb tense and modal forms used.

  EXAMPLE: You need a questionnaire. A questionnaire _____*is needed.*_____

1. Last week, I surveyed twenty people.

  Last week, twenty people _____

2. I gave questionnaires to the respondents.

  Questionnaires _____

3. I recorded their answers.

  Their answers _____

4. We have compiled the results.

  The results _____

5. We will publish a report soon.

  A report _____

6. Every day, companies conduct surveys.

  Every day, surveys _____

7. They must carefully plan the survey questions.

The survey questions _____

8. Yesterday, a polling firm released the results.

Yesterday, the results _____

9. The public should have ignored the results.

The results _____

T I P

Be in the Passive Voice

In the passive voice, sometimes the verb *be* is suggested but not written. The following sentence contains the passive voice.

> (which was)
> The survey, conducted in 2009, had shocking results.

EXERCISE **7**

Underline and correct eight errors with the passive voice.

> found
> EXAMPLE: A problem was <u>find</u> with the design.

1. When the Apple computer company first released the Macintosh, a pull-down menu was include in the product. The computer also had a variety of icons for different tasks. For instance, useless files were drag to a trash can icon. A year later, Microsoft Corporation introduced its popular software program name Windows 2.0. The software, modify in 1988, looked a lot like Apple's software. Apple sued Microsoft for copyright infringement and argued that Microsoft had copied the "look and feel" of Apple software.

2. There are strict rules about copyright. A unique product can be patent. However, people cannot copyright an idea. Therefore, Apple's decision to use specific icons could not be protect. Still, Apple argued that its original concept should not have been copy. The case, which lasted for four years, was win by Microsoft.

Answer the following questions. If necessary, go back and review the appropriate section.

1. Add an -s or -es ending, where needed.

   a) Everybody sing_____.

   b) Two-thirds of the people sing_____.

   c) No one sing_____.

   d) Both of my friends sing_____.

   e) Neither of us sing_____.

   f) Either Jay or Muriel sing_____.

   g) One of my friends sing_____.

   h) My brothers sing_____.

2. Underline and correct the error in each sentence.

   a) The work was complete by an independent contractor.

   b) He wanted to be pay under the table.

   c) The owner, along with his two brothers, have a lot of money.

   d) There is many illegal practices in the construction industry.

FINAL REVIEW

PART A

Write the correct verb in the space. The verb may be active or passive.

EXAMPLE: Last March, the case (discuss) ___*was discussed*___ in our business ethics class. Nobody (be) ___*was*___ absent that day.

1. The book *Marketing: Real People, Real Choices* (publish) _____ in 2008. According to author Michael Solomon, of the more than 17,000 new products launched each year, 25 percent (be) _____ new brands. In marketing, one of the most important ingredients (be) _____ a product's name. Thus, every brand name (choose) _____ with care by a team of specialists.

2. Product names should be impressive. Irish Spring, as well as Nike and Olay, (be) _____ memorable. However, every year some marketing mistakes (make) _____ . For example, in 1990, the company Toro called its lightweight snow blower the Snow Pup. The product (sell) _____ in hardware stores across the nation. When polled, 25 percent of the population

(be) _____ not impressed with the name. A year later, the

product (rename) _____ Snow Master and then Snow

Commander. Now, the product, with its new name, (be) _____

very successful.

PART B

Underline and correct ten errors with agreement or voice.

EXAMPLE: In a survey, members of the public were _asked_ ~~ask~~ which brands they buy.

3. Statistics shows that most people are influence by brand names. Some popular brands

such as Kleenex, Jell-O, Scotch tape, and Kool-Aid has become the product name

in consumers' minds. Everybody are familiar with those products. However, a

company can lose its trademark if a brand name falls into "common usage." There is

some examples that show the problem. In the past, both kerosene and yo-yo was

the names of specific brands. Currently, each of those words refer to the product,

not the brand. Those names can no longer be trademarked.

4. The company Kimberly-Clark, which manufacture

Kleenex, does not want the word _Kleenex_ to replace

the word _tissue_. One of the company's ads contain

the line "Would you like a tissue?" Someone else

reply, "I won't use any tissue. I only use Kleenex brand."

UNIT 11

GERUNDS AND MODIFIERS

 Using the -ing Form

The *-ing* form of the verb can function in the following ways. In this chapter, you will practise using the *-ing* form when it functions as a gerund and as a modifier.

Progressive verb: I am **reading**. I was **working** yesterday when you called.

Adjective: It was an **inspiring** sight. She had a **frightening** experience.

Modifier: **Working** hard, I hoped to get a promotion.

Subject gerund: **Exercising** is vital for the health. **Listening** is an important skill.

Object gerund: He denied **taking** the money.

EXERCISE 1

Fill in the blanks with one of the words from the list. Use the *-ing* form of each verb. If you don't understand the meaning of the word, use your dictionary.

bicker	crush	drill	nudge	splash
bounce	dip	grab	smear	sprinkle

EXAMPLE: _____*Bouncing*_____ the ball, the athlete planned to make a jump shot.

1. After _____ for days, the rig worker suddenly heard the oil gush to the surface.

2. _____ me with his foot, Adam drew my attention to the _____ couple.

3. _____ paprika, the chef added the colourful spice to his creation. Then he realized he had forgotten to add garlic. He considered _____ a clove of garlic with a small hammer.

4. _____ cream on her face, Jamilla examined the lines under

her eyes. Then, _____ her fingertips into the jar of face cream,

she considered her options.

5. _____ her purse, Jamilla headed for the door.

 # Gerunds and Infinitives

Sometimes a main verb is followed by another verb. The second verb can be a gerund or an infinitive. A **gerund** is a verb with an *-ing* ending. An **infinitive** consists of *to* and the base form of the verb.

> Verb + gerund: The accountant <u>denied</u> **stealing** the money.
> Verb + infinitive: He <u>agrees</u> **to discuss** it.

■ Some Verbs Followed by Gerunds

acknowledge	deny	keep	recollect
admit	detest	loathe	recommend
adore	discuss	mention	regret
appreciate	dislike	mind	resent
avoid	enjoy	miss	resist
can't help	escape	postpone	risk
can't stand	finish	practise	
consider	imagine	quit	
delay	involve	recall	

You should <u>consider</u> **meeting** the new secretary.
We <u>recommend</u> **sleeping** eight hours a night.

■ Some Verbs Followed by Infinitives

afford	deserve	manage	seem
agree	expect	mean	struggle
appear	fail	need	swear
arrange	guarantee	offer	tend
ask	happen	plan	threaten
choose	have	prepare	volunteer
claim	hesitate	pretend	wait
compete	hope	promise	want
dare	intend	refuse	wish
demand	learn	resolve	would like

We <u>chose</u> **to meet** at a later date.
I <u>promise</u> **to inform** you about any problems.

■ Some Verbs Followed by Gerunds or Infinitives

Some common verbs can be followed by gerunds or infinitives. Both forms have the same meaning.

begin	continue	like	love	start

Mr. Kim <u>started</u> **to speak**. Mr. Kim <u>started</u> **speaking**.
(Both sentences mean the same thing.)

■ Prepositions Followed by Gerunds

Prepositions are often followed by a gerund. Review the following patterns.

Verb + preposition:	I <u>insist</u> on **driving** you.
Be + adjective + preposition:	We <u>are</u> responsible for **closing** the store.
Verb + object + preposition:	Nothing <u>prevents</u> him from **running** for office.

■ Some Common Words Followed by Prepositions plus Gerunds

accuse of	(be) fond of	(be) responsible for
(be) accustomed to	forbid *her* from★	succeed in
apologize for	forgive *me* for★	take part in
(be) capable of	(be) good at	think about
complain about	insist on	think of
discourage *him* from★	(be) interested in	(be) tired of
dream of	look forward to	warn *me* about★
(be) enthusiastic about	(be) nervous about	(be) worried about
(be) excited about	prevent *him* from★	
feel like	prohibit from	

★Certain verbs can have a noun or pronoun before the preposition.

EXERCISE 2

Underline the correct words in parentheses.

EXAMPLE: We hope (<u>to visit</u> / visiting) the employment centre.

1. I am interested (to work / <u>working</u> / in working) at your company. I dream (to be / of being) a cartoonist, and I adore (to use / using) animation software. During the past five years, I have managed (to learn / learning) about the best animators. In my college, I never failed (to read / reading / on reading) about the most recent advances in technology. I have considered (to try / trying / at trying) another profession, but I always come back to my art.

2. In my spare time, I enjoy (to illustrate / illustrating) short graphic novels. I also have a part-time job. At a pet shop, I am responsible (to clean / for cleaning) the cages. I never complain (to do / about doing) hard work. In fact, I am prepared (to give / giving) all of my energy and attention to my career.

3. I look forward (to meeting / to meet) you at your earliest convenience. I would appreciate (to have / having) a chance to explain what my goals are. I am very good (to solve / solving / at solving) problems, so I believe I will be a great asset to your team.

Sincerely,
Marcus J. Bloom

■ Special Forms

Some verbs can be followed by either a gerund or an infinitive, but there is a difference in meaning depending on the form you use.

Term	Form	Example	Explanation
need	+ infinitive	He needs <u>to phone</u> his son.	*Need* is usually followed by an infinitive.
	+ gerund	Your hair needs <u>cutting</u>.	When *need* has a passive meaning, use the gerund. The sentence means "his hair needs to be cut."
remember	+ infinitive	Please remember <u>to feed</u> the cat.	Remember to perform a task.
	+ gerund	I remember <u>meeting</u> you before.	Have a memory about a past event.
stop	+ infinitive	She stops <u>to buy</u> gas every week.	Stop an activity (driving) to do something else.
	+ gerund	She stopped <u>smoking</u> last week.	Permanently stop doing something.

TIP

Used To

Be careful with *used to*. Notice the differences in meaning in the following examples.

- *(be) used to* + gerund means "accustomed to."

    I <u>am used to</u> **staying** awake at night.

- *used* + infinitive expresses a past habit.

    When I was a child, I <u>used</u> **to hide** under my bed.

EXERCISE **3**

Underline the correct words in parentheses.

> EXAMPLE: As a child, I used (<u>to scream</u> / to screaming) when I did not get what I wanted.

1. Do you remember (using / to use) a typewriter? Before computers were common, most people were used (to type / to typing) on a manual or electric typewriter. When they made a mistake, they had (to redo / redoing) the page again.

2. A secretary named Bette Graham was tired (to make / of making) mistakes when she typed. As an amateur artist, she was used (to think / to thinking) outside of the box. Graham was used (to work / to working) with acrylic paints, and she knew that she could paint over errors on a canvas. One day, Graham decided (to mix / mixing) some paint to make it the colour of her stationery. Then she started (to type / typing) a page. A minute later, she stopped (to type / typing) and pulled the paper out of the typewriter. Then she applied some of the paint over the typed ink. It masked the ink perfectly.

3. The next day, when she went to work, Graham remembered (bring / to bring) the small paint bottle with her. That day, whenever she made an error, she stopped (to type / typing) and she applied the paint to the paper. Later, when she was about to leave the office, she stopped (to tell / telling) some co-workers about her invention. They were excited and asked her (to bring / bringing) more bottles of paint to work.

4. Graham went home and created "Mistake Out" labels for her bottles. Graham knew that she needed (to protect / protecting) her idea. She remembered (to patent / patenting) her invention so that nobody else would steal her idea. Bette Graham succeeded (to create / in creating) a million-dollar company. The next time you use a product called Liquid Paper, remember (to thank / thanking) Bette Graham!

EXERCISE 4

Underline and correct errors with gerunds and infinitives. Write "C" next to correct sentences.

EXAMPLE: The boss discussed to hire a new warehouse worker. *hiring*

1. A month ago, Philippe Roy hoped finding a new job.

2. At a warehouse, the manager decided to give Philippe a job.

3. Philippe was not used to lift heavy objects, and on the second day he hurt his back.

4. He risked to lose his job if he didn't get in better shape.

5. To improve his health, he decided going to a gym.

6. Philippe disliked to work out, but he knew that he had to build up his strength.

7. Every morning, after he finished to exercise at the gym, he headed to the warehouse.

8. He doesn't regret joining a health club.

9. Now he appreciates to have good health.

10. Philippe stopped to be lazy, and now he manages to exercise daily.

Modifiers

A **modifier** is a word, a phrase, or a clause that modifies—or describes—another element in the sentence. To use a modifier correctly, place it next to the word(s) that you want to modify.

    modifier   words that are modified
Working alone, <u>the artist</u> made an immense mural.

Only combine sentences using an *-ing* modifier when the two actions happen at the same time.

    Separate sentences: The pianist closed his eyes. He played the song beautifully.
    Combined sentences: **Closing his eyes**, the pianist played the song beautifully.

Combine the sentences by converting one of the verbs into an *-ing* modifier. There may be more than one way to write the sentence.

EXAMPLE: The pop art movement began in the 1960s. It incorporated media images.

Incorporating media images, the pop art movement began in the 1960s.

Beginning in the 1960s, the pop art movement incorporated media images.

1. Andy Warhol worked as an illustrator. He drew footwear for a shoe company.

_____

_____

2. He wanted to be taken seriously as an artist. He approached an art gallery.

_____

_____

3. The gallery owner rejected Warhol's art. She wanted original ideas.

_____

_____

4. Warhol felt inspired. He decided to create pop art.

_____

_____

5. Warhol needed an original idea. He focused on his favourite brands.

_____

_____

6. He reproduced soup cans and Coke bottles. He attracted a lot of attention.

_____

_____

■ Misplaced and Dangling Modifiers

A **misplaced modifier** is a word, a phrase, or a clause that is not placed next to the word that it modifies.

Misplaced: I suddenly saw an amazing painting **walking in the museum**.
(Can a painting walk in the museum?)

Always place a modifier near the item that it modifies.

Correct: **Walking in the museum**, I suddenly saw an amazing painting.

A **dangling modifier** does not modify any words in the sentence. It "dangles" or hangs loosely because it is not connected to anything in the sentence.

Dangling: **To view the exhibit**, a pass is required.
(Who is viewing the exhibit?)

Ensure that your modifier has an item to modify.

Correct: **To view the exhibit**, <u>members of the public</u> need a pass.

EXERCISE 6

Correct the misplaced or dangling modifier in each sentence.

EXAMPLE: [∨]Tamara de Lempicka studied art <u>filled with excitement</u>.
Filled with excitement,

1. Tamara developed a love of drawing who was talented.

2. Painting daily, the images became more and more powerful.

3. Clients paid Tamara very well who wanted a portrait.

4. She made a painting of herself in a green car which won an award.

5. She was able to buy a château loved by admirers.

T I P

Using *Enough*

Enough should be placed after verbs, adjectives, and adverbs. However, it should be placed before nouns.

After a verb:	I did not <u>eat</u> **enough** yesterday.
After an adverb:	I did not work <u>quickly</u> **enough**.
After an adjective:	The child is not <u>old</u> **enough** to take the train alone.
Before nouns:	There are not **enough** <u>people</u>. Do you have **enough** <u>money</u>?

EXERCISE 7

Correct the misplaced or dangling modifier or look for errors with *enough*. You may need to add or remove words to ensure that the sentence makes sense. Write "C" next to correct sentences.

EXAMPLE: The girl[∨]dropped her purse <u>who was in the front row</u>.
, who was in the front row,

1. The music students put on a show who are at the top of their classes.

2. To get accepted into the music program, immense talent is required.

3. Also, students must be enough old to handle the heavy training schedule.

4. On Saturday, with great pride, Mario Goya performed difficult classical pieces of music.

5. When he sat at the piano, he wondered if he had practised enough hard.

6. For his final song, Mario concentrated on the piano keys wearing a serious expression.

7. After performing, the audience was thanked.

8. Mario retreated to his dressing room in a blue robe.

9. He talked to some fans removing his makeup.

10. Mario did not earn enough money for his performance.

UNIT Review

Answer the following questions. If necessary, go back and review the appropriate section.

1. What is a gerund? _____

2. Correct the mistake(s) in the following sentence.

Make decisions and manage people are my strengths.

3. Circle five verbs that should be followed by a gerund.

prepare	risk	enjoy	pretend	wait
finish	learn	choose	practise	delay

4. Underline the appropriate answer in parentheses.

I regret (using / to use) my cellphone during working hours. I risk (to lose / losing) my job. I really need (working / to work) and can't afford (finding / to find) another job. I hope (meeting / to meet) with the manager. I would like to apologize (to be / for being) unprofessional.

5. Identify and correct any misplaced or dangling modifiers.

a) She works with oil paint wearing silk shirts.

b) After finishing a painting, the brushes should be cleaned.

PART A

Underline the correct answer in parentheses.

EXAMPLE: I am used (to wait / waiting / <u>to waiting</u>) until the last minute.

1. Can you imagine (to create / creating) a bestselling product? Many ordinary

people are capable (to have / having / of having) fabulous ideas. They would like

(to become / becoming) wealthy inventors.

2. Julie Clark, the founder of the Baby

Einstein Company, was used

(reading / to read / to reading) to

her child. She also wanted her baby

(to watch / watching) good videos.

She remembered (to read / reading /

of reading) a psychology book when

she was in college several years

earlier. According to the book, children need (to be / being) stimulated with music.

She thought (to show / showing / about showing) her baby some videos with

classical music and interesting characters, but none existed. She stopped (to look /

looking) for a commercial video and decided (to create / creating / for creating)

her own.

3. Clark went to her basement and finished (to film / filming) a video in two days.

She managed (to sell / selling) copies of her "Baby Einstein" and "Baby Mozart"

videos to family and friends. Within a year, her little business was responsible

(to generate / generating / for generating) over $100,000 in profits. Five years later,

Clark succeeded (to sell / selling / in selling) her company to Disney for millions

of dollars. However, some pediatricians publicly declared that videos are not good

for babies, so in 2007 Disney stopped (to use / using) the word "educational" in

its marketing material.

4. (Start / To start / Starting) a home business can be a risky but rewarding endeavour.

If someone decides to invent a product, he or she should remember (to do / doing)

some research. Experts recommend (to hire / hiring) a marketer to find out if consumers want the product. Also, budding inventors must be proactive and stop (to procrastinate / procrastinating). They should be enthusiastic (to do / doing / about doing) the project. The most passionate and hardworking inventors can succeed.

PART B

Identify misplaced modifiers and mistakes in the placement of *enough*. You may need to add or remove words and modify punctuation to ensure that the sentence makes sense. There are five errors.

EXAMPLE: ^{Drinking tea,} I planned a public service announcement <u>drinking tea</u>.

5. Rafael made a video about drinking and driving. He rented his camera at a local store which turned out to be defective. He hired his friends to perform in the video as a driver and a pedestrian saving money. After he was sure that he had spent enough time working on the project, he presented it to his classmates. In the video, teenagers learn about safe driving who want to be responsible. For presentation day, Rafael projected his video on a large screen, and the audience applauded loudly. Doing great work, the video was impressive. However, he wasn't enough confident to consider filmmaking as a career.

UNIT 12

NUMBERS AND MECHANICS

 Numbers

There are two basic styles for number usage. Business and technical writing have one style, and academic writing has another. **In business and technical fields**, use numerals instead of words in charts, statistics, graphs, financial documents, and advertising. The numbers *one* to *ten* are written as words only when they appear in sentences.

However, **in academic writing**, numbers are spelled out more often. Review these rules for using numbers in academic writing.

- Spell out numbers that can be expressed in one or two words:

  > We spent **eleven** days in Vancouver.
  > There were **forty-seven** job applicants.
  > The airline had room for **four hundred** passengers.
  > That day, **thousands** of people cleared customs.

- Use numerals with numbers of more than two words.

  > The manager booked rooms for **358** guests.

- When the sentence begins with a number, spell out the number. If the number has more than two words, do not place it at the beginning of the sentence. (You can add *About* or *Exactly* before the number.)

  > **Three hundred** people were invited to the concert.
  > There were **158** guests.

- Spell out fractions and hyphenate them.

  > Only **one-third** of the respondents own a house.

- Use a numeral before *million* or *billion*, but spell out *million* or *billion*. (It is easier to read *20 million* than *20,000,000*.)

  > The company hopes to sell about **14 million** units.

- Use numerals when writing measurements, addresses, dates, times, degrees, pages, or divisions of a book. Also use numerals with prices and percentages. (For prices, you can use the *$* symbol or write *dollars*. Notice that the symbol appears before the number.)

  > A yearly subscription costs **$29**, which is about **15** percent less than the cover price.

T I P

Several Numbers in a Sentence

When writing two consecutive numbers, write out the shorter number.

We used two 14-inch pieces of glass.

Be consistent when writing a series of numbers. If some numbers require numerals, then use numerals for all of the numbers.

We ordered 19 desks, 8 filing cabinets, and 120 paper packages.

EXERCISE 1

The following sentences appeared in academic writing. Correct any errors with numbers.

EXAMPLE: Pat Ray was just _nine_ 9 years old when she picked up a camera.

1. 100 students were invited to a photography exhibit, and 2/3 decided to go.

2. In her studio, Patricia Ray has six oil paintings, 112 photographs, and thirty-three watercolours.

3. She has worked professionally as an artist for 10 years.

4. A small art gallery exhibited 25 of Ray's watercolours.

5. 40 people came to the art exhibit.

6. Ray would like to publish an art book and sell each book for one hundred and twenty-nine dollars.

7. She wants to self-publish 50 168-page books.

8. In a survey, ninety-five percent of respondents called Ray's photographs "exceptional."

9. 689 people viewed the exhibit after paying the 10$ admission fee.

10. Some Picasso artworks have sold for over 30,000,000 dollars.

 # Abbreviations

An **abbreviation** is the shortened form of a word. Sometimes a Latin abbreviation is used for common words. For instance, *i.e.* means *id est* in Latin, or "that is" in English.

Dr. = Doctor   Mr. = Mister   p.m. = *post meridiem* (after noon)

Other types of abbreviations (also known as **acronyms** or **initialisms**) are formed with the first letters of a group of words. Many companies and organizations use such abbreviations.

OPEC = Organization of Petroleum Exporting Countries

EXERCISE 2

Write out what each abbreviation means.

EXAMPLE: Feb. _____February_____

1. e.g. _____
2. Mrs. _____
3. apt. _____
4. Ave. _____
5. Blvd. _____

6. Ltd. _____
7. Corp. _____
8. Inc. _____
9. lb _____
10. Jr. _____

EXERCISE 3

Write the long form of each abbreviation.

EXAMPLE: FBI _Federal Bureau of Investigation_____

1. RCMP _____
2. AIDS _____
3. CSIS _____
4. CEO _____
5. NAFTA _____
6. R.I.P. _____

Capitalization

Most capitalization rules apply to specific individuals or places. If you make a general reference without giving a specific name, capitalization is unnecessary.

a doctor   a street   the school   the company

Always capitalize the following:

- The pronoun *I*
- The first word of every sentence

- The days of the week, the months, and holidays

    Thursday   June 15   Labour Day

    Note: Do not capitalize seasons: *spring, summer, winter, fall.*

- The names of buildings, streets, parks, public squares, lakes, rivers, cities, provinces, and countries

    Manulife Building   Regent Boulevard   Mount Royal Park
    Lake Louise   Red River   Winnipeg, Manitoba

- The names of companies, schools, and colleges

    Apple Computer   Morrow High School   Franklin College

- Languages, nationalities, tribes, races, and religions

    Swiss   Mohawk   Catholic

- The titles of specific individuals

    General Dallaire   Prime Minister Brown   Doctor Morrow

- The first word and all major words in titles, excluding articles (*a, an, the*), prepositions (*in, on, at,* etc.), and conjunctions (*and, but, or*)

    Great Expectations   *Lord of the Flies*   *Prison Break*

- The names of historical events, eras, and movements

    World War II   Pleistocene Era   The Jazz Age

- The complete and official names of government or academic departments

    Department of Modern Languages   Centre for Rural Affairs

T I P

Courses, Degrees, and Programs

Courses

Only capitalize the names of courses when you refer to the official title.

> No caps: This semester, I am taking courses in **c**hemistry, **p**hysics, and **b**iology.
> Caps: I have **B**iology 201 today and **C**hemistry 100 tomorrow.

Degrees

Do not capitalize academic degrees when spelled out. Only capitalize the abbreviated form.

> No caps: Mike has a **m**aster of **a**rts in literature.
> Caps: Mike has an **M.A.** in literature. He wants to get a **Ph.D.** later.

Programs

Do not capitalize names of programs or areas of study.

> She is studying **a**rt, and her minor is in **m**usic. He is in the **h**umanities.

EXERCISE 4

Add fifteen missing capital letters to the following paragraphs.

1. The New York academy of sciences has examined how people respond to music. The study, done in april of 2005, examines whether musical training can make people smarter. The researchers found that listening to a song such as Radiohead's "fake plastic trees" can enhance brain functions.

2. Gordon Shaw earned his bachelor of science and later completed a doctorate in physics at cornell university. He was co-founder of the Music Intelligence neuronal development institute. He also wrote the book *Keeping Mozart in mind*. Shaw studied the link between music and the brain. He determined that music can enhance math abilities.

3. I wish I had known about Shaw's theories when I studied in math at Greendale high school. I would have studied with the song "Tonight's the night" playing on my headphones. Maybe I will study music in university.

Punctuation

■ The Apostrophe (')

Use an apostrophe to form contractions.
- Join certain subjects and verbs together. They**'re** busy.
- Join an auxiliary to *not*. He should**n't** quit his job.

The apostrophe is also used to indicate possession.
- Add *'s* to singular nouns, even when the noun ends in *-s*. Ann**'s** dog and Jess**'s** cat
- Add an apostrophe after the *-s* on plural nouns. the worker**s'** lockers
- Add *'s* to irregular plural nouns. the men**'s** room

■ The Comma (,)

Use a comma

- with quotations (after an introductory phrase or before an end phrase);
  Gandhi said**,** "Fear kills the soul."
  "Fear kills the soul**,**" Gandhi said.

- to separate words in a series. Generally place a comma before the final *and*;
  Everyone needs food**,** water**,** and shelter.

- in a date (before the year), when the order is month, day, and year. If the date comes in the middle of a sentence, put a comma after the year;
  John Lennon was born on October 9**,** 1949**,** and died on December 8, 1980.

- after an introductory word or phrase;
  After the election**,** the candidate rested.

- after a transitional expression;
  However**,** we may meet later.
  The judge made her decision; therefore**,** the case is closed.

- around interrupting phrases that give additional information about the subject;
  Isabelle**,** an artist**,** makes astonishing paintings.

- in compound sentences before the coordinator (*and, but, yet, or, so*);

    The job is easy, but it doesn't pay very well.

- around relative clauses containing *which*;

    The files, which are in my office, contain important information.

- around relative clauses containing *who*, when the *who* clause contains non-essential information.

    No comma: The woman who stole my car was arrested.
    (The information in the *who* clause is essential in order to understand the sentence.)

    Comma: Marilyn Reed, who is from Calgary, stole my car.
    (You can understand the sentence without the *who* clause.)

TIP

Comma Usage

Some people mistakenly believe that a comma's role is to show pauses. However, a comma has a more specific function: it helps to keep distinct ideas separate. Never separate a subject from its verb with a comma.

There were many reasons the company's president⟍ decided to flee the country.

■ The Semicolon (;)

Use a semicolon

- to connect two related and complete thoughts;

    The company has closed; about fifty people lost their jobs.

- to connect items in a series if the items have internal punctuation or are very long.

    The presentations will be in Calgary, Alberta; Winnipeg, Manitoba; Houston, Texas; and Seattle, Washington.

■ The Colon (:)

Use a colon

- after a complete sentence that introduces a quotation;

    Seth Godin gives his views about success: "Leaders must be willing to fail."

- to introduce a series or a list after a complete sentence;

    Someone who grieves passes through five stages: denial, anger, bargaining, depression, and acceptance.

- to introduce an explanation or example;

    The tiny painting is outrageously expensive: it costs $1.5 million.

- after the expression *the following*;

    Please do the following: read, review, and respond.

- to separate the hour and minutes in expressions of time.

    The exhibit will open at 12:15.

Correct twenty punctuation errors. You may need to add, change, or remove some punctuation marks.

EXAMPLE: Scientists examine human brains/ to learn about creativity.

1. Can signs of genius, be observed in peoples brains? When Albert Einstein was about age three his parents brought him to a pediatrician. Albert seemed to be very bright, however he could not talk.

2. Children usually learn to speak as follows recognition, mimicry, production, and fluency. At the time, Mrs. Einstein did not understand Alberts problem so, she was frustrated with her son.

3. On a Friday at 2h15, the Einstein's were shocked when Albert began to speak. Later, the boy surprised his teachers, because he could do complicated equations. Whenever, the boy had a chance, he made mathematical formulas.

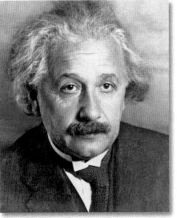

4. Albert Einstein offered to give his brain to scientists, before he died. In 2003, Dr. Kenneth Heilman examined a piece of Einstein's brain, he recorded his findings. Dr. Heilman, who works at the University of Florida wrote about the study. He discovered that the esteemed scientist, had unusual brain development. The left side of Einstein's brain which developed slowly, may have influenced the right hemisphere's growth. The differences in Einstein's brain, may have played a critical role in his intelligence according to Dr. Heilman.

The following sentences appeared in student writing. Fix twenty punctuation and capitalization errors.

1. I dislike philosophy. Although, I think it will be useful for my personal culture.

2. Gabriella went to High School in Lachine, then she came to our college two years ago.

3. I will finish my Music courses this year, and Gabriella will finish her's next year.

4. After losing a job, people go through several stages; anger, denial, hope, and action.

5. Working with the public is fine, because the job requires it.

6. The students answers were divided, some will graduate in march and other's in december.

7. Karine want's to get a Degree in Science.

8. Karine likes her courses however, she wants to change programs next year.

9. Three things she likes are: psychology, math, and french.

UNIT Review

Answer the following questions. If necessary, go back and review the appropriate section.

1. Correct the number errors in each sentence.

   a) About twenty percent of the population loves his paintings.

   b) 40 people were at the show.

   c) We spent a hundred dollars on the painting.

2. Correct the punctuation errors in each sentence.

a) The house which had been renovated, was extremely beautiful.

b) For Andre, the most important things in life are: love, money, and fame.

c) Karine's classes are in the same building as her three friends classes.

FINAL REVIEW

Identify and correct fifteen errors in numbers, capital letters, or punctuation.

EXAMPLE: Richard Avedon was a photographer of/ people, places, and things.

1. Richard Avedon a great fashion photographer, grew up in New York. Avedon lived on 74th avenue and went to University in the city. At Columbia university, he studied Philosophy. Later, he decided to become an artist.

2. In his twenties, Avedon became a staff photographer for *Vogue*, he also worked for *Harper's bazaar*. Many of Avedons photos featured three items a chair, a white backdrop, and a face. Generally, all of his model's faces are lit up with stark lighting.

3. In 1976, Avedon published a book called *Portraits*. His book has 29 fashion shots, 125 portraits, and twelve war images. One of his photos, an iconic image of Marilyn Monroe has been reproduced in 1000s of books and magazines.

4. On october 1, 2004, Richard Avedon passed away. Before he died, he compared photography to music "The way I see is comparable to the way musicians hear."

EDITING PRACTICE

Practise editing student writing. The exercises in this unit contain a wide variety of errors.

EXERCISE 1

Underline and correct twenty errors in the student paragraph. Editing symbols indicating the types of errors to be found in each line appear in the margin. To understand the meaning of each symbol, look at the Editing Guide on the inside back cover of this book.

C / SP / VT	In my english class, I met someone with a nice personnality who's born in Montreal.
WF / VT / SV	My partner name is Vincent. He choose to study at our college because he want to earn
C / P / SV	a diploma in Commerce. He likes this program, because there is no science courses.
P	The other things he likes in the program are: the teachers and the friendly students.
F	Also, his main strengths. They are in math and computers. Furthermore, he is very
WC / SP / //	sportif. His weaknesses are his lazyness, his procrastination, and he is shy. In the future,
O / WF	he would like to travel because he never been outside his province. His hobbies are play
RO	video games and exercising, he also plays piano. Ultimately, Vincent hopes to get a
WF / SP / WF	bachelor degree in commerce and to open his own compagny. He has very realist goals.

EXERCISE 2

Underline and correct fifteen errors in the student writing sample. Editing symbols indicating the types of errors to be found in each line appear in the margin. To understand the meaning of each symbol, look at the Editing Guide on the inside back cover of this book.

WC / WF	To have a healthy diet, ensure that you make the good choices. First, avoid to eat red
WF	meat. It is preferable having lean meat such as ham or chicken. Also, proteins can be
SP / WC	found in fish, wich has less calories than meat and contains omega–3 fatty acids.
WF	Moreover, you should have five to 10 portions of fruit and vegetables per day. Every
P / P	time, you have a chance include fruits and vegetables in your diet. Cut the amount of
VT / WF / RO	sugar you ate because it can leads to belly fat, it is bad for blood pressure. For example,
O / WO	instead eating cake, consider fruit salad. Do you know what is the recommended amount
	of sugar? You should just have four to six spoons per day. Finally, remember that too much
DS	salt it can cause high blood pressure in some adults. According to HealthCastle.com,
P	you should "either cut or halve the amount of salt called for in recipes".

Underline and correct the errors in the sentences. The type of error is indicated in bold. Then write a rule for each error. The first rule has been done for you.

1. **Tense:** Two weeks ago, a survey has been distributed.

Rule: *When an action was completed at a known past time, use the past tense.*

(See pages 70 to 73 in Unit 8 for more information about tenses.)

2. **SV agreement:** Over 40 percent of the population rarely buy bottled water.

Rule: _____

(See page 91 in Unit 10 for more information about agreement and percentages)

3. **Comparison:** The youths have more better knowledge about Facebook then the older respondents.

Rule: _____

(See page 17 in Unit 2 for more information about comparatives.)

4. **Run-on:** Most of the males do not exercise daily, the females are also lazy.

Rule: _____

(See page 41 in Unit 5 for more information about run-ons.)

5. **Fragment:** The targets: forty college students.

Rule: _____

(See page 41 in Unit 5 for more information about fragments.)

6. **Modifier:** When asked the survey questions, the results were a mess.

Rule: _____

(See page 105 in Unit 11 for more information about dangling modifiers.)

7. **Embedded question:** Respondents were asked how can children be encouraged to stay in school.

Rule: _____

(See page 64 in Unit 7 for more information about embedded questions.)

8. **Conditional:** If the surveyors would have polled more people, the answers would have been more relevant.

Rule: _____

(See page 85 in Unit 9 for more information about conditionals.)

The following letter contains ten errors. Correct six punctuation errors and four capitalization errors.

Dr. Ahmed Rahim

33 Winestead road,

Victoria BC VIA 2L2

May 6 2010

Nicole Robitaille

965 Woodstock street

Fredericton, NB E3C 2K0

Subject, Research Assistant Position

Dear ms. Robitaille

I have received your application for a position as a research assistant. Unfortunately, there are no openings at this time. Please accept my apologies. Your education and experience appear exemplary.

Respectfully Yours

Dr. A. Rahim
Dr. Ahmed Rahim

Underline and correct twenty-five errors in this student research essay written by Stephanie Saumur.

1. These days, its common to see someone holding his cellphone while walking, driving, or having dinner. This new technology it has became essential to our way of life. In fact, there are about 100 millions cellphone users. Many researches on this gadget been done, which reveal that cellphone microwaves might have impact on human health.

2. Cellphone emissions have positive and negative effects on concentration and memory. The positive effect is that cellphones microwaves can help humans memorize things. In the other hand, a study was done to observe the long-term memory of rats after exposing them to cellphone microwaves. University of Washington researcher Henry Lai put rats in water, and they tried to find a platform. He discovered that cellular radiation affect their spatial reference because rats that were exposed had more problems finding the platform than the one that weren't exposed. Australian scientists discovered that radiation from cellphones "can slow reaction time" in humans. (Szalavitz) Such radiation can also be responsible of other problems.

3. The link between cellphones and brain damage or cancer is controversial. John Moulder, a professor of radiation biology at the Medical College of Wisconsin, do not believe that cellphones cause brain cancer. However, Kjell Mild, a professor of biology, thinks that there is clear links between cancer and cellphones. Regarding brain cancer, he says: "If you look at the studies with large numbers of people who used mobiles for ten years or more, all show an increased risk" (Szalavitz). Moreover, researcher Paolo Rossini, concluded that microwaves have an impact on the cortex. Ground-braking research shows that cellular radiation affects the blood-brain barrier, according to a Finnish study, it "might cause brain tissue damage" (Fletcher).

4. In conclusion, scientists do not agree if cellphones are positives or negatives. Have you a cellphone? Experts suggest wearing a hands-free equipment to reduce symptoms and health problems that cellphones may cause.

IRREGULAR VERB LIST

Base Form	Simple Past	Past Participle	Base Form	Simple Past	Past Participle
arise	arose	arisen	feed	fed	fed
be	was, were	been	feel	felt	felt
bear	bore	borne/born	fight	fought	fought
beat	beat	beat/beaten	find	found	found
become	became	become	flee	fled	fled
begin	began	begun	fly	flew	flown
bend	bent	bent	forbid	forbade	forbidden
bet	bet	bet	foresee	foresaw	foreseen
bind	bound	bound	forget	forgot	forgotten
bite	bit	bitten	forgive	forgave	forgiven
bleed	bled	bled	forsake	forsook	forsaken
blow	blew	blown	freeze	froze	frozen
break	broke	broken	get	got	got/gotten
breed	bred	bred	give	gave	given
bring	brought	brought	go	went	gone
build	built	built	grind	ground	ground
burst	burst	burst	grow	grew	grown
buy	bought	bought	hang	hung/hanged	hung/hanged
catch	caught	caught	have	had	had
choose	chose	chosen	hear	heard	heard
cling	clung	clung	hide	hid	hidden
come	came	come	hit	hit	hit
cost	cost	cost	hold	held	held
creep	crept	crept	hurt	hurt	hurt
cut	cut	cut	keep	kept	kept
deal	dealt	dealt	kneel	knelt	knelt
dig	dug	dug	know	knew	known
do	did	done	lay	laid	laid
draw	drew	drawn	lead	led	led
drink	drank	drunk	leave	left	left
drive	drove	driven	lend	lent	lent
eat	ate	eaten	let	let	let
fall	fell	fallen	lie[1]	lay	lain

1. *To lie* means "to rest or lie down on a sofa or bed. "When *lie* means "make a false statement," then it is a regular verb: *lie, lied, lied*.

Base Form	Simple Past	Past Participle	Base Form	Simple Past	Past Participle
light	lit	lit	slide	slid	slid
lose	lost	lost	slit	slit	slit
make	made	made	speak	spoke	spoken
mean	meant	meant	speed	sped	sped
meet	met	met	spend	spent	spent
mislead	misled	misled	spin	spun	spun
mistake	mistook	mistaken	split	split	split
mow	mowed	mowed/mown	spread	spread	spread
overdraw	overdrew	overdrawn	spring	sprang	sprung
overtake	overtook	overtaken	stand	stood	stood
pay	paid	paid	steal	stole	stolen
prove	proved	proved/proven	stick	stuck	stuck
put	put	put	sting	stung	stung
quit	quit	quit	stink	stank	stunk
read	read	read[2]	strike	struck	struck
rid	rid	rid	strive	strove	striven
ride	rode	ridden	swear	swore	sworn
ring	rang	rung	sweep	swept	swept
rise	rose	risen	swell	swelled	swollen
run	ran	run	swim	swam	swum
say	said	said	swing	swung	swung
see	saw	seen	take	took	taken
sell	sold	sold	teach	taught	taught
send	sent	sent	tear	tore	torn
set	set	set	tell	told	told
shake	shook	shaken	think	thought	thought
shed	shed	shed	throw	threw	thrown
shine	shone	shone	thrust	thrust	thrust
shoot	shot	shot	understand	understood	understood
show	showed	shown	wake	woke	woken
shrink	shrank	shrunk	wear	wore	worn
shut	shut	shut	weep	wept	wept
sing	sang	sung	win	won	won
sink	sank	sunk	wind	wound	wound
sit	sat	sat	withdraw	withdrew	withdrawn
sleep	slept	slept	write	wrote	written

2. The past forms of *read* are pronounced "red."

APPENDIX 2

COMBINING IDEAS IN SENTENCES

MAKING COMPOUND SENTENCES

A

Complete idea

, coordinator
, and
, but
, nor
, or
, so
, yet

complete idea

B

Complete idea

;

complete idea

C

Complete idea

; transitional expression,
; furthermore,
; however,
; in fact,
; meanwhile,
; moreover,
; therefore,

complete idea

MAKING COMPLEX SENTENCES

D

Complete idea

subordinator
although
because
before
even though
unless
when

incomplete idea

E

Subordinator
Although
Because
Before
Even though
Unless
When

incomplete idea

,

complete idea

© PEARSON LONGMAN • REPRODUCTION PROHIBITED

124 GRAMMAR GOALS

APPENDIX 3

SPELLING AND GRAMMAR LOGS

On the next pages, or in the first few pages of your writing portfolio or copybook, try keeping two "logs" to help you avoid repeating errors and to improve your writing.

■ Spelling Log

The goal of keeping a spelling log is to stop repeating errors. Every time you misspell a word, record both the mistake and the correction in your spelling log. Then, before you hand in a writing assignment, consult the list of misspelled words.

Incorrect	Correct
finaly	finally
responsable	responsible

■ Grammar Log

The goal of keeping a grammar log is to stop repeating errors in sentence structure, mechanics, and punctuation. Each time a writing assignment is returned to you, identify one or two repeated errors and add them to your grammar log. Next, consult the grammar log before you hand in new writing assignments in order to avoid making the same errors. For each type of grammar error, you could do the following:

1) Identify the assignment and write down the type of error.

2) In your own words, write a rule about the error.

3) Include an example from your writing assignment.

> Cover letter (Mar. 10): Fragment
> Sentences must have a subject and verb and express a complete thought.
> Also, my enthusiasm. ~~That~~ helps me stay focused.

ⓐ Spelling Log

Errors	Corrections

◖ Grammar Log

INDEX

abbreviations **110–111**
academic and business language
   1–10
accept or *except* **22**
active or passive voice **93–95**
actually or *currently* **22**
adjectives **15, 16–18, 99**
  –comparative/superlative **17–18**
  –no plural form **15**
  –with *-ing* ending **99**
adverbs **16–17**
  –comparative/superlative **17–18**
  –frequency **67**
advice or *advise* **22**
affect or *effect* **22**
aloud or *allowed* **22**
animator, group leader, or *host* **27**
apostrophes **113**
appositives **49**
as ... as, the same as **17**
audience and purpose **7–8**

brackets **54**

capitalization **111–113**
clauses (types of) **41**
collective nouns **89**
colon **114**
combining sentences **42–46**
  –with subordinators **42**
  –with *who, that, which* **45–46**
comma **42, 43, 45, 113–114**
commonly confused words
   22–23
concise english **4**
conditionals **85–87**
connotation **3–4**
conscience or *conscious* **22**
consistency (tenses) **76–77**
council or *counsel* **22**

deceived or *disappointed* **27**
denotation **3–4**
doctor or *medicine* **28**

double negatives **2**

either ... or and *neither ... nor* **63**
ellipses **54**
embedded questions **64**
enough (placement) **105**
except or *accept* **22**
experiment or *experience* **27**

false cognates **27**
faulty logic (avoiding) **44**
few, fewer, or *fewest* **18**
for or *since* **24**
formation or *background* **28**
fragments **41**
frequency adverbs **67**
future perfect tenses **72**
future tenses **70**
  –in conditional forms **85**
  –time clauses **71**

gerunds **89, 99–103**
  –as subjects **89, 99**
  –following verbs **100–101**
good and *well* **17**

hope or *wish* **84**

indefinite pronouns **12, 89, 91**
infinitives following verbs **100**
irregular verb list **118–119**

jargon **8**

many, few, fewer, fewest **18**
modals **82–84**
  –chart **82**
  –*must* and *have to* **82**

modals and mood **82–88**
modifiers **103–108**
  –defined **103**
  –misplaced and dangling
   104–108
mood **84–86**
  –conditionals **85–87**
  –hope or wish **84**
  –necessity or demand **84**
much, little, less, least **18**

non–count nouns **15**
numbers **109–110**

organism or *organization* **28**

parallel structure **61–64**
paraphrasing **57**
passive voice **93–95**
past perfect tenses **72, 85**
past tenses **70, 85**
personal or *personnel* **22**
phrasal verbs **25–26**
phrase (defined) **40**
plurals **14–15**
possessive forms of nouns
prefixes meaning "not" **32**
prefixes, scientific roots, and
   suffixes **31–32**
prepositional expressions **25**
prepositions **24, 91–92, 101**
  –before gerunds **101**
  –in subject-verb agreement
   91–92
  –*since* or *for* **24**
  –*to* **24**
present perfect **71**
present perfect progressive **71**
present tenses **70, 85**
principal or *principle* **22**
pronouns **11–13, 45, 89, 91**
  –antecedent agreement **11**
  –avoiding *I* and *you* **13**
  –indefinite pronouns **12, 89, 91**
  –pronoun shift **13**
  –pronouns in comparisons **11**

Notes